thirty-two short films about glenn gould

thirty-two short films about
GLENN GOULD

François Girard and Don McKellar

A RHOMBUS MEDIA PRODUCTION

COACH HOUSE PRESS

To our non-consenting collaborator:
we hope you're not disappointed.

© François Girard, Don McKellar
and Rhombus Media, 1995
Photos © Cylla von Tiedemann, 1995

Coach House Press
760 Bathurst Street, 2nd floor
Toronto, Canada
M5S 2R6

FIRST EDITION
1 3 5 7 9 8 6 4 2
Printed in Canada

Published with the assistance of the Canada
Council, the Ontario Arts Council and the
Department of Canadian Heritage.

Canadian Cataloguing in Publication Data
Girard, François, 1956–
Thirty-two short films about Glenn Gould :
   the screenplay
ISBN 0-88910-493-X
1. Gould, Glenn, 1932-1982 — Drama.
I. McKellar, Don. II. Title.
PN1997.T5 1995   791.43'72   C95-931947-6

Contents

INTRODUCTION

I was seventeen in 1958 and I had a friend who was an aspiring pianist. His idols were Arthur Rubinstein and Vladimir Horowitz. One day he confided to me in a conspiratorial tone that a young pianist from Toronto was coming to town next month. His concert was not going to be advertised in the papers or anywhere else. This artist did not need advertisement, people just knew where and when he would be playing.

One snowy evening in March I took the tramway across town to the old Her Majesty's Theatre. The hall was packed to the rafters with people who looked like they were waiting for the Second Coming. On the bare stage there was a Steinway raised on wooden blocks with an old Persian rug under the pedals and a battered chair hardly higher than a foot-stool.

The lights came down and a very pale, twenty-five-year-old man walked nonchalantly onstage with his hands in his pockets. With a self-mocking smile he whispered that by popular request he had just decided to change his programme and that instead of a partita and a sonata he would play *The Goldberg Variations*. The audience gasped. He then very quickly lowered himself onto his old chair, blew on his fingers and attacked the first Variation at a staggering speed. Now at that point in my life I had never heard *The Goldberg Variations*. Listening to them for the first time played live by Glenn Gould is a little bit like losing your virginity with Marilyn Monroe: you never entirely recuperate from it. His dazzling virtuosity, his astounding sense of rhythm and his overall intelligence were positively stunning. I sat there with my mouth open, transfixed. I had never and would never again in my life hear someone play the piano that well except maybe Thelonious Monk very late one night in a very smoky nightclub. (But that would be another story).

When I heard that François Girard was working on a Glenn Gould script, I was rather sceptical. Gould had described himself as a Puritan. And Puritans seldom make very good film characters. English-Canadian artists are a strange lot. Probably because of the fact that their country is so profoundly hostile to art, they feel the need to hide themselves behind a facade of absolute banality. Alex Colville looks, speaks and dresses like the C.E.O. of a large accounting firm. Glenn Gould could easily have been mistaken for a slightly disheveled Presbyterian minister. David Cronenberg could pass for an Oshawa engineer. And yet what strange passions lurk behind these inscrutable masks. I have always found great English-Canadian artists to be incredibly lonely, disturbed and dangerous people. That is why they are so interesting. Colville's overriding angst and his morbid fascination for guns upset me a lot more than Francis Bacon's simplistic literalism. But then what can you say about people like that? How can you explain that the best pianist in the world suddenly stops playing and starts to make strange radio shows exploring the loneliness of people living under the Arctic circle? What can you say about a world-famous artist who is so desperately in need of human warmth that he is reduced to using the personal -ads section of the newspapers? Physically and spiritually we inhabit an incredibly bleak country. That is why the first scene of *Thirty-Two Short Films About Glenn Gould* is so poignant. This is the very good script that gave birth to a very good film. It does not try to explain, it does not analyse. It simply beholds the mystery of creation.

DENYS ARCAND
NOVEMBER, 1995

THIRTY-TWO SHORT FILMS ABOUT GLENN GOULD

(ARIA)

EXT. DAY. A NORTHERN EXPANSE.

The endless white of the Far North. The opening aria of Bach's *Goldberg Variations* can be heard faintly over the whistling wind. A small black dot appears at the centre of the distant horizon. At first it appears to be still, but gradually we recognize movement. Over the next few minutes the shape begins to grow until it has defined the image of a man walking towards us. As he approaches, the music grows clearer.

The man is Glenn Gould. We recognize him by his dark coat, his hat, his habit of hiding his hands and by the way he rounds his shoulders. He reaches us and stops. Standing on the desert of frozen rubble, he surveys the world before him.

The music fades away.

LAKE SIMCOE

EXT. AFTERNOON. THE SUMMER HOME.

The Overture from Wagner's *Tristan and Isolde* begins to play. We are looking out over a lake, and then the camera moves slowly towards a comfortable cottage. Glenn Gould's father is raking leaves.

INT. AFTERNOON. THE SUMMER HOME.

Sunday afternoon. The modest decor—bare wood, knick-knacks and conscious rustic charm—is subordinated to the beloved piano, which is clearly the heart of the living room, if not of the family.

Voice-over begins. We see young Glenn Gould, age three, sitting on his mother's knee so he can reach the keyboard. With one finger extended to its fullest, he takes a deep breath and strikes a key. Completely engrossed, he listens to the resounding note with almost religious concentration. When the last overtones have completely died away, he turns to his mother. She smiles and nods to him encouragingly.

> G.G.
> [*voice-over*]
> *My mother tells me that by five years old I had decided*
> *definitively to become a concert pianist.*
> *I think she had decided sometime earlier.*
>
> *The story goes that while I was in the womb she played the*

piano continuously, to give me a head start. And, evidently,
it paid off.

My mother was my first teacher and I've never doubted her
methods. After all, she introduced me to Bach. By the age of
ten I had the first book of The Well-Tempered Clavier
pretty much under my belt.

The voice-over continues as young Glenn leans his ear closer to the
soundboard and deftly strikes the same key again. Another tone rings.
He listens intently, eyes filled with wonder, as it too dies away. And
again. We feel that this has likely been going on for some time.

G.G.
[*voice-over*]
My childhood was full of music even at our cottage on Lake
Simcoe. Those days seem particularly idyllic to me, at least in
retrospect. They certainly were, compared to my school days.

The voice-over ends. We move away from the scene and out through
the window.

EXT. LATE AFTERNOON. LAKE SIMCOE.

The sounds of the solitary notes still ring clearly.

We are looking the other way now, facing the lake. We pass through a
curtain of birch trees to find a boy sitting in a deck-chair on the dock.
A rowboat is moored nearby.

The voice-over resumes and, simultaneously, we hear a child's voice
come drifting to us over the still water.

G.G.
[*voice-over*]
At an early age, I could read music and memorise it on the
spot. In fact I could read music before I could read words.

CHILD'S VOICE
... 9 x 9=81, 9 x 10=90, 9 x 11=99, 9 x 12=108, 9 x
13=117, 9 x 14=126, 9 x 15=135, 9 x 16=144, 9 x
17=153, 9 x 18=162 ...

The multiplication table is recited with astonishing confidence. We are
quite sure that it is the voice of Gould as a child, but we must wait a
little longer for confirmation. The frame tightens in on the boat and the
child sitting in the chair. Meanwhile, the fog and the half-light prevent
us from seeing the face of the child clearly.

CHILD'S VOICE
... 34 x 57=1938, 34 x 58=1972, 34 x 59=2006, 34
x 60=2040, 34 x 61=2074, 34 x 62=2108, 34 x
63=2142, 34 x 64=2176, 34 x 65=2210 ...

G.G.
[voice-over]
*I remember, I used to play a game with my mother where I
would identify the chords she played from the other side of
the house.*

*People always seem to make a great deal out of these early
signs but they hardly constitute miracles, in my opinion. I
simply have a facility with a certain kind of minutia. I
always have.*

EXT. DAY. BOY SITTING IN CHAIR ON DOCK.

Now we are right up close to this child who is hypnotised by his own
recitation. Gould is several years older now. The manner and bearing are
nascent but indisputable.

G.G.
... 87 x 23=2001, 87 x 24=2088, 87 x 25=2175, 87
x 26=2262, 87 x 27=2349, 87 x 28=2436, 87 x
29=2523, 87 x 30=2610 etc....

The Wagner slowly fades up under the scene.

EXT. NIGHT. SUMMER HOME.

Gould's father is collecting wood from the wood pile. He carries it towards the house.

INT. NIGHT. SUMMER HOME.

The voice-over resumes as we move into the living room. Gould's mother is pressed against the wall beside the door frame. She stands motionless, a magazine held against her body, listening intently to what's going on in the next room. Gould's father steps into view and is just about to speak when his wife holds up her hand to silence him.

> G.G.
> [*voice-over*]
> *I often think how fortunate I was to have been brought up in an environment where music was always present. Who knows what would have become of me otherwise. It's a question I often ask myself. But, I've yet to come up with an answer.*

Through the door to the next room, we find a still older Glenn Gould, lit by a lamp, enraptured by the symphony broadcast. He leans into the radio as the Wagner swells to a climax. There is a tear in his eye.

FORTY-FIVE SECONDS AND A CHAIR

Forty-Five Seconds and a Chair *is based on a photograph in* Non, je ne suis pas du tout un excentrique *by Glenn Gould, translated by Bruno Monsaingeon, Fayard Publishers, p. 96.*

INT. DAY. A LIVING ROOM.

The Two Part Invention #13 from Bach's *Two and Three Part Inventions* begins to play. Completely immobile, Glenn Gould is seated in an antique leather chair. He is well supported, his legs crossed, his fingers interlaced. From the first second of this scene, it is his fixed, concentrated gaze into the camera that captures our attention.

In the background is a long window hung with sheer curtains. The floor is covered in bare wood that runs to a series of old radiators lining the wall beneath the window.

We move slowly towards Gould. There is nothing else but this slow camera movement. We continue advancing until we have come close enough to challenge the strength of Gould's gaze. Gould's gaze continues for a few more seconds. The music stops. He closes his eyes.

BRUNO MONSAINGEON

musician and collaborator

Bruno Monsaingeon is a musician, writer and filmmaker. He collaborated with Gould on a regular basis over a period of ten years. Out of this collaboration emerged seven one-hour television programs which presented Gould's work. Monsaingeon is also responsible for most of the French translations of Gould's work.

EXT. DAY. PARIS.

Hanging perilously over the roofs of the city, we see a view of Paris from Montmartre. Here and there, the regular lines formed by these roofs are broken by the outline of a cathedral.

EXT. DAY. A BALCONY/PARIS.

Bruno Monsaingeon is seated on a balcony that overlooks the city. The distant outlines of Paris float behind him as he speaks about Glenn Gould.

> MONSAINGEON
>
> Je l'ai vu, après tout, la première fois dans un hôtel à Toronto lorsqu'on s'est rencontrés pour la première fois après de multiples palabres au téléphone; ou par lettre pour prendre notre premier rendez-vous. Je l'ai rencontré, il faisait 30 degrés à l'extérieur, il faisait vraiment très chaud. Il était en manteau, il avait sa casquette, des écharpes, des gants enfin tout un accoutrement qui semblait extravagant et qui en réalité correspondait exactement à la protection qu'il avait besoin, dont il avait besoin vis-à-vis du monde extérieur pour se protéger de ce qui en fait il est mort, des ... des ... des problèmes de germination, des problèmes de tension sanguine. Donc, si vous voulez, la première vision qu'on pouvait avoir de quelqu'un de ce genre était très très étonnante. On ne

pouvait pas ne pas être saisi devant quelqu'un avec cet air quasiment clochardesque. Souvent il entrait dans votre chambre à l'hôtel et puis il y restait pendant 18 heures d'affilée. Aucun souci extérieur, aucun souci de la nourriture ou quoique ce soit ne venait troubler en fait le rapport qu'on est en train d'établir. Et la seconde chose qui vous ait frappé, c'était l'humour, c'était l'extraordinaire capacité de s'amuser et de lancer … de lancer des idées qui étaient stimulantes à la fois par leur profondeur et par leur drôlerie. Donc, vous savez cette manière un petit peu bizarre qui était la première chose que vous saisissiez et qui ne durait que cet instant de la première rencontre, après c'était fini. Ça disparaissait très rapidement pour faire place à l'homme réel qu'il était … qui était. En fait, rien chez lui ne cherchait à choquer. Ç'était tout simplement lui-même qu'il cherchait à exprimer.

SUBTITLES

The first time I saw him was in a hotel in Toronto, where after numerous telephone calls and letters we agreed to meet face-to-face. It was 30°C outside, really hot ... but he had on a coat, hat, scarf and gloves! It was an extravagant get-up but it provided him the kind of protection he needed from what in the end would kill him ... infection, high-blood pressure, etc. so, with someone like that, your first impression is one of shock. I couldn't help but be taken aback by his hobo-like appearance. Often he would come to my hotel room and stay for 18 hours at a stretch. He had no concern for the outside world or food or anything not related to the rapport we were developing. I was also struck by his humour ... the extraordinary ability he had to enjoy himself and to throw out ideas as profoundly stimulating as they were funny. So this bizarre impression you had on first meeting him lasted only a moment and was gone. It was replaced by an impression of the real man who didn't in any way seek to shock but simply to express himself.

GOULD MEETS GOULD

text by Glenn Gould

In the February 1974 edition of High Fidelity *magazine (p. 72), there appeared an article entitled 'Glenn Gould Interviews Glenn Gould About Glenn Gould', a part of which is included in* Gould Meets Gould.

INT. DAY. A RECORDING STUDIO.

Bach's Prelude from *English Suite #5* begins to play, and a man's voice is heard in the darkness, through which we can barely perceive the abstract shapes of microphones, cables and recording equipment. His tone suggests that of an interviewer. A few seconds later, a face attaches itself to this voice in the darkness as a silhouette appears from nowhere. We can see nothing but the outline of the man's body as he sits with his legs crossed. Nevertheless, the profile and attitude are enough to bring to life the memory of Glenn Gould.

G.G.

Mr. Gould, to begin with, let me ask straight-out: Are there any off-limit areas?

Another figure appears out of the darkness and prepares to answer the question that has been posed. This new figure walks slowly in the gloom. As we hear his voice it is clear that he is also Glenn Gould and that this interview is between Gould and himself.

G.G.

I certainly can't think of any ... apart from music of course.

G.G.

Well, Mr. Gould, I don't want to go back on my word. I realize that your participation in this interview was never

contractually confirmed but I had rather assumed that we'd
spend the bulk of this interview on musically related matters.

G.G.

Do you think it's essential? I mean my personal phi-
losophy of interviewing—and I've done quite a bit of
it on the air as you perhaps know—is that the most
illuminating disclosures derive from areas only indi-
rectly related to the interviewee's line of work.

G.G.

For example?

G.G.

Well, for example, in the course of preparing radio
documentaries, I've interviewed a theologian about
technology, a surveyor about William James, a house-
wife about acquisitiveness in the art market ...

G.G

But surely you've interviewed musicians about music?

G.G.

Well, yes I have, on occasion, in order to help put
them at ease in front of the mike. But it's been far
more instructive to talk with Leopold Stokowski , for
example, about the prospect for interplanetary travel
which is, and I'm sure you'll agree ...

G.G.

*Let me put it this way: is there a subject you'd particularly
like to discuss?*

G.G.
[*standing still*]
What about Native rights in Alaska?

G.G.

Well, I must confess I had a rather more conventional line of attack, so to speak, in mind, Mr. Gould. As I'm sure you're aware, the virtually obligatory question in regard to your career is the controversy which you created by giving up live concert performance at the age of 32, choosing only to communicate through the media. I do feel we must at least touch on it.

G.G.

[*walking slowly*]

As far as I'm concerned, it primarily involves moral rather than musical considerations. In any case be my guest.

G.G.

Well now, you've been quoted as saying that your involvement with recording—with media in general, indeed—represents the future ...

G.G.

That's correct.

G.G.

... and that conversely the concert hall, the recital stage, the opera house or whatever, represent the past: an aspect of your own past in particular perhaps as well as, in more general terms, music's past.

G.G.

That's true.

G.G.

I hope you'll forgive me for saying that these ideas are only partly justified. Also, I feel that you, Mr. Gould, have foregone the privilege, that is rightfully yours, of communicating with an audience ...

G.G.

... from a power base?

33

G.G.

... from a setting in which the naked fact of your humanity is on display, unedited and unadorned.

G.G.

Couldn't I at least be allowed to display the tuxedoed fallacy, perhaps?

G.G.

Please Mr. Gould, I don't feel we should let this conversation degenerate. I've tried to pose the question in all candour and ...

G.G.

Well then, I'll try and answer likewise. To me, the ideal audience-to-artist relationship is a one-to-zero relationship, and that's where the moral objection comes in.

G.G.

Run that by me again.

G.G.

First, I'm not at all happy with words like 'public' and 'artist'; I'm not happy with the hierarchical implications of that kind of terminology. The artist should be granted anonymity. He should be permitted to operate in secret, as it were, unconcerned with—or better still, unaware of—the presumed demands of the marketplace, which demands, given sufficient indifference on the part of a sufficient number of artists, will simply disappear. And given their disappearance, the artist will then abandon his false sense of 'public' responsibility, and his 'public' will relinquish its role of servile dependency.

G.G.

And never the twain shall meet!

G.G.

[passing slowly behind the seated Gould]
No, they'll make contact, but on an altogether more meaningful level.

G.G.

[turning to face the passing Gould]
Mr. Gould, I'm well aware that this sort of idealistic role swapping offers a satisfying rhetorical flourish. The 'creative audience' concept to which you've devoted a lot of interview space elsewhere offers a kind of McLuhanesque fascination. But you conveniently forget that the artist, however hermetic his lifestyle, is still in effect an autocratic figure. He's still, how-ever benevolently, a social dictator. [becoming more and more excited] *And his public, however generously enfran-chised by electronic options, is still on the receiving end of the experience. And all your neo-medieval anonymity quest on behalf of the artist-as-zero and all of your vertical pan-cultur-alism on behalf of his 'public' isn't going to change that!*

G.G.

May I speak now?

G.G.

Of course, I didn't mean to get carried away, but I do feel strongly about the ...

G.G.

... about the artist as Superman?

G.G.

That's not quite fair, Mr. Gould.

G.G.

... or about the interlocutor as comptroller of con-versation, perhaps?

G.G.

There's no need to be rude!

35

A silence interrupts the dialogue. The two Goulds face each other. One standing, the other seated, they study one another and then turn away.

                    G.G.
        What about this? If you imagine that the artist is to
        be ...

The music ends.

HAMBURG

EXT. DAY. DOWNTOWN HAMBURG.

A small pleasure-boat engine is heard through the mist that hangs over the waters of Hamburg's inner lake. The imposing facade of the Vier Jahreszeiten hotel rises proudly from the right bank. We hear Glenn Gould's voice, filtered through a telephone, speaking haltingly.

> G.G.
> [*off-camera*]
> Yes ... that's right ... Toronto ... Toronto, Canada. It should read as follows:

INT. DAY. GLENN GOULD'S HOTEL ROOM/HAMBURG.

As he talks on the phone, a young Glenn Gould turns away from the window and busily scans the headlines of a newspaper. He walks around the room, obviously enjoying himself in the luxurious suite. A chambermaid is cleaning the room

> G.G.
> Dear Walter—stop—Under the weather yesterday—stop—X-rays reveal chronic bronchitis ... bronchitis in right lung—stop—feeling as foggy as it is outside—stop—Little comfort from dubious doctor—stop—he would suit you perfectly—stop—concerts tomorrow and Monday cancelled, can not and will

not leave this room—stop—End.

INT. DAY. HALLWAY OF THE VIER JAHRESZEITEN HOTEL.

A porter walks down the luxurious corridor with a package in his hand. He stops in front of Room 318 and knocks. He is received by Gould, dressed in wool and wearing gloves. The phone receiver is still tucked under Gould's chin. Through the opening of the door we can see the chambermaid finishing up her work in the room.

> PORTER
> [*thick German accent*]
> Sir, I am sorry to disturb, but we have a parcel ...

> G.G.
> From New York?

> PORTER
> Yes sir.

> G.G.
> Yes, at last. Excellent. [*he takes the package with enthusiasm*] Thank you ... Bye ... Danke.

The porter turns to go. Gould stops him with an upraised hand, tucks the package under his arm and digs a generous tip out of his pocket. The porter accepts it with a little bow. Gould closes the door.

> G.G.
> [*into the phone*]
> Yes that would be it, indeed. Could you read it back to me please?

INT. DAY. THE HOTEL ROOM.

Gould crosses the floor, anxiously unwrapping the package. He talks into the phone.

40

G.G.

[*to the phone*]

... No, no. I ... concerts tomorrow and Monday can-
celled, of course—not can't sell. That means something entirely different.

The chambermaid is finished. Gould stops her before she can leave.

G.G.

Wait, wait ... please stay.

Gould escorts her back into the room. He gestures for her to sit in an
armchair in the centre of the room.

CHAMBERMAID

Aber mein herr, entschuldigung ich muss arbeiten.

Gould again gestures for her to sit. He takes the record he has
unwrapped over to the gramophone and sets it up, drawing the curtains
over the window.

G.G.

[*still talking into the phone*]

No ... go ahead ... Yes. ... that's absolutely flawless.
Could you send it off immediately, please. Room 318.
Thank you.

He hangs up. There is a moment of awkward silence. Gould turns to
face the chambermaid. She seems somewhat uncomfortable, wonder-
ing what he is about to do. Keeping his eyes on her, he backs over to
the record player and drops the needle. Suddenly, there is a miraculous
outpouring of music. The music fills the room with a rush of emotion,
unmistakably Beethoven.

The Allegretto from *Sonata #13* is heard with all its nostalgic candour.
Gould, however, remains unconvinced. He steps behind the armchair
and lowers himself to the chambermaid's ear level. After listening
intently for a moment or two, he crosses back to the phonograph and
delicately adjusts the treble and bass knobs. Then it's back behind the

41

chair for another listen. This time he seems satisfied. He sits behind the maid.

The chambermaid has now completely given up on her schedule and resigned herself to this odd presentation. As the music plays, her anxiety is gradually allayed and her apprehensions are translated into curiosity. She examines her obliging captor and submits herself to the music. Gould, in turn, watches his audience. He holds his breath so as not to disturb the flow of the music.

Suddenly, she looks directly at him. As he watches, she rises and picks up the record cover. Her suspicions are confirmed when she sees Gould's picture on the sleeve. She looks back to him. Their eyes meet and lock. In respectful silence, she turns away and walks slowly to the window. Gould awaits the judgement. The chambermaid pulls herself together and offers him her hand.

The music comes to an end.

CHAMBERMAID
Danke schoen.

VARIATION IN C MINOR

A BLACK SCREEN.

A short, passionate movement from Beethoven's *32 Variations in C Minor* begins. Two vertical white lines appear on the black screen, vibrating in sync with the music. These are the two channels from the optical track of the film. There is no other image. The music holds solitary reign.

PRACTICE

INT. NIGHT. THE GREEN ROOM OF A CONCERT HALL.

Glenn Gould enters and begins to walk the floor of his backstage rehearsal space. He flips through a score for Beethoven's *Tempest*. After a moment he tosses the music onto a couch. He turns off the nearby light.

G.G.

[*voice-over*]

... Salzburg to Stockholm, Berlin, Wiesbaden, Florence, Tel Aviv, Jerusalem, and on the whole tour, I'd say there were maybe six good hotel rooms, five comfortable beds and, at least, three adequate pianos.

Some of these pianos were so hopelessly unwieldy I decided it was best just to ignore them. It required a kind of mystical transcendence to get me through. I have no idea what the audiences resorted to.

I'm not one of those piano freaks, you know. Of course, I'm aware there are people who would gladly sit in the most uncomfortable chairs with three thousand other people in uncomfortable chairs, and listen to hours and hours of the stuff, but it's nothing I would ever subject myself to. I just don't like the sound of piano music that much.

Suddenly we hear a rich passage of music, Beethoven's Allegretto from

Sonata #17 (The Tempest). Gould plays along on an invisible keyboard. His fingers dance, and as the music grows so do his gestures. He moves about the room, expressively conducting the imaginary music.

The camera begins to circle Gould, faster and faster, like a whirlwind tethered to his dancing hand. The whirlwind ends with the conclusion of the music.

Gould has moved to a piano in the centre of the room. He closes the keyboard cover and turns to leave.

THE L.A. CONCERT

INT. NIGHT. DRESSING ROOM.

Backstage in an old concert hall. Downtown Los Angeles.

The dressing room is slightly run-down but spacious and comfortable.
Glenn Gould is leaning over the sink with his shirt sleeves rolled up,
soaking his hands and wrists in warm water. There is a knock on the
door. A young female voice calls out.

GUIDE

Five minutes, Mr. Gould.

Gould closes his eyes.

INT. DAY. BACKSTAGE CORRIDORS.

The guide is outside the dressing-room door, speaking on a house
phone. As she is talking, the dressing-room door opens and Gould steps
out dressed for the concert.

GUIDE
[into the phone]

Yeah, you can tell him to close the doors now. Yeah,
I think he's ready ... I told you, go ahead. Ah! Here
we come.

She hangs up the phone and addresses Gould, smiling graciously.

> GUIDE
>
> This way Mr. Gould.

She leads Gould down the hall. Gould holds his hands, reddened from soaking in hot water, protectively close to his chest. The concert promoter appears and tags along to one side.

> PROMOTER
>
> Glenn, I didn't want to bother you now but I'm not gonna be here after the show.

> G.G
>
> That's fine.

> PROMOTER
>
> Gary's gonna be here. Don't think about it; the guy with the short ... you know. He's gonna pick you up. Oh! and there is a reception after ... Yeah, I know, it's gonna be squaresville man but you would make a couple of grey-haired ladies really happy, if you'd just waltz through one time, you know. I did wanna show you your schedule for tomorrow. No, no ... No, don't bother with it, don't bother with it now, don't even think about it. But if you have a moment after, you wanna change anything ...

> G.G
>
> I'm sure it's fine.

We reach an elevator door at a fork in the corridors. The guide presses the 'up' button.

> PROMOTER
>
> ... you wanna see more of L.A. ... I'm gonna leave it on your dresser.

G.G.

Thank you.

The girl smiles and presses the button a second time.

GUIDE

Maybe we should take the stairs.

G.G.

Maybe we should.

PROMOTER

Don't even think about it now.

The promoter drops back. Gould and his guide climb an old stairwell.

GUIDE
[apologizing meekly]

It's a long way.

G.G

It certainly is. If it weren't for you I would have been dropping bread crumbs along the way.

The guide leads Gould through a door to the stage level. The hum of the audience is heard. Gould is ushered into the dark wings of the grand old stage. Along the way they pass that floor's closed elevator door, where a frustrated technician repeatedly pushes the buttons. Inside, an elderly stage hand gets up from his post and hands the guide a flashlight.

Leaving Gould, the guide drops back to speak to someone. After a moment the stage hand removes his headset and tentatively approaches Gould with a pen and programme.

STAGE HAND

Mr. Gould ...?

55

                        G.G.
Of course.

Gould takes the pen and paper and starts to write.

                    STAGE HAND
My wife has all of your records.

                        G.G
Well, tell your wife that she has exceptional taste. Also,
she is very lucky. I'm never going to sign one of these
again. How long have you worked for this theatre?

                    STAGE HAND
It's been almost 30 years.

                        G.G
Thirty years. You must be near retirement, if you don't
mind my asking?

                    STAGE HAND
No, at the end of the season.

                        G.G
What will you do after that?

                    STAGE HAND
Well, I have my garden.

                        G.G.
Yes?

                    STAGE HAND
I'm going to build an arboretum. You know what that
is?

                        G.G
I think so, yes.

The sound of the crowd has settled down. The house lights are lower-
ing. The guide, who has been waiting at some distance, takes advantage
of this break in the conversation and unobtrusively steps in.

GUIDE

Mr. Gould?

Gould nods to the guide and turns back to the man. He finishes writ-
ing and hands back the paper.

G.G

My best to your wife and garden.

STAGE HAND

Thank you.

Gould steps away and takes a moment to collect himself. He nods to
the guide and she lights his way to the break in the curtain. Gould steps
through and the hushed audience bursts into applause. The guide turns
to the stage hand who is studying the autograph.

GUIDE

What did he say? What did he write?

STAGE HAND

'April 10, 1964, best of luck on your new career.
Glenn Gould ... The Final Concert.'

They both look out on the stage. The audience is applauding, antici-
pating the opening chord.

CD 318

INT. DAY. PIANO.

The roar of a crowd, carried over from the previous scene, slowly
fades away.

As the first note of Bach's Prelude #2 from *The Well Tempered Clavier* is
heard, we find ourselves within the piano itself. The camera studies the
minute workings of the piano's interior; the flying hammers, the
dampers rising and falling, the strings vibrating when struck.

Gradually we move out of the piano and study its exterior—the gleam
of varnished wood, the gold Steinway plate and the serial number, CD
318, that identifies the Steinway that Gould preferred over all others.
The music ends.

Beginning from a close-up of the piano's exterior—the entire frame
filled with the wood of the piano's side—we begin a slow dolly away
from the piano, moving towards the back of the stage. Gradually it is
revealed that the immense auditorium is completely empty. The camera reaches the back of the stage as two workmen in coveralls move into
frame and begin to gently cover the piano and move it offstage.

The lights in the auditorium shut off, one by one.

YEHUDI MENUHIN

violinist

Like Glenn Gould, Yehudi Menuhin won wide early renown for his virtuosity and toured extensively as a young man, but from there their careers sped off on wildly divergent courses. He and Gould had a unique relationship. Aside from the affinity which bonded their friendship and exceptional talent, the two men enjoyed many differences of opinion.

INT. DAY. BERGEN.

Yehudi Menuhin is seated in front of a window. The rooftops of Bergen and the surrounding mountains are seen in the background.

> MENUHIN
>
> Je crois que comme toute personne essaie de justifier leur position, font ce qu'ils veulent faire de toute façon mais veulent encore justifier d'une façon universelle, lui aussi est tombé dans ce piège, ce piège où il exagérait un peu la moralité de sa décision. Evidemment, il avait, d'un certain point de vue, raison. Dans un public, il y a ceux qui entendent mieux, ceux qui entendent moins bien, ceux qui voient mieux, ceux qui voient moins bien. Quelquefois il y a des spectateurs dans les grandes églises qui sont assis derrière des piliers, qui ne voient rien. L'accoustique quelquefois est exagérée, ou on entend quelque chose de trop ou de trop peu ou, c'est … le volume est trop grand ou la réverbération qui fait mal aux oreilles. Il a raison, ce n'est pas toujours idéal et … et ça fait partie de la vie. Pour moi, ça existe comme élément vivant. La vie de Glenn Gould, je trouverais presque personnellement, trop, trop artificielle pour moi. Mais, comme je dis, c'est parce que je ne suis pas de sa taille; du point de vue créateur, je ne peux pas me faire une vie tout … tout seul àl'exclusivité, excluant

tout le reste du monde et ne faisant, me concentrant
que sur cet exercise intellectuel et physique et
essayant d'échapper à tous les courants d'air protégé
par un foulard, ne pouvant pas supporter que
quelqu'un me touche à l'épaule. En même temps il
adorait aller dans les villages des pêcheurs dans les
grandes. ... comment? ... dans les distances qu'offre
le Canada; ça il aimait. La nature, il l'aimait. Les
hommes naturels, il les aimait. Il aimait le pêcheur
beaucoup plus qu'un public à New York.

SUBTITLES

I think that, like all people who try to rationalize their position
—who do what they want, but seek some sort of universal
justification—he fell into a trap in that he somewhat overex-
aggerated the morality of his decision. Of course, from a
purist's stance, he had a point. In a concert hall, some people can hear or see better than others. Sometimes, in large
churches people are seated behind pillars and can't see. The
acoustics may be exaggerated ... something may be too loud
or not loud enough. The volume is too loud, or the reverbera-
tion hurts your ears. He was right, it's not always ideal. But
that's part of life. For me, that exists as a living element. I per-
sonally would find Glenn Gould's life too artificial. For me. But
like I said, that's because I'm not of his artistic stature as a
creator. I could not lead a life completely isolated ... completely cutting off the rest of the world, doing nothing but
applying myself to the intellectual and physical work, trying to
avoid every draft behind a scarf, unable to bear someone
touching my shoulder. Yet, at the same time he loved to go to
the fishing villages in the great ... How do you say? ... in the
wide expanses Canada has to offer. He liked nature. He liked
real people. He liked fishermen far more than the audiences
in New York.

PASSION ACCORDING TO GOULD

INT. DAY. A RECORDING STUDIO.

We recognize the recording studio we saw in *Gould Meets Gould*. Glenn Gould sits at a piano, removing a blood-pressure cuff from his arm.

INT. DAY. A RECORDING BOOTH.

A tape reel spins madly. We hear the contents of the tape at high speed and backward. The tape stops abruptly as a mechanism catches the spool and blocks its motion. We see a scrawled label on the tape spool which reads: G.G. – 12/1/63. Voices are heard over the intercom.

PRODUCER

Ready?

ASSISTANT ENGINEER

Yeah!

INT. DAY. A RECORDING STUDIO.

PRODUCER
[*off-camera*]

Glenn, we're ready for playback here. I'm gonna give
it to you without E.Q.-ing, O.K.? And all the levels

are flat. Ready in 3 ... 2 ... 1.

Gould is sitting at the piano in the middle of tripods, sound screens and rows of cable that run to the piano. He turns his young face towards the voice and indicates his approval with a slow gesture. He is calm and dreamy; we feel his exhaustion at the end of a long session. The studio is dark, and once more we see Gould only as a silhouette. The first bars of Bach's Gigue from *English Suite #2* are heard. Attentive, Gould stands, totters slightly and lets loose a series of involuntary gestures.

INT. DAY. BOOTH.

The music continues as, inside the cluttered control booth, we find three weary, shirt-sleeved men. The producer seems fairly satisfied, nodding along with the music. He watches Gould through the window. The engineer is in the worst shape. He slumps down in his chair, a newspaper is spread out on the board in front of him.

ASSISTANT ENGINEER

Coffee?

PRODUCER

Yes ... Yes.

The assistant engineer exits.

INT. DAY. STUDIO.

A spectacular movement, fiery with passion and consummately played, follows the slow opening of Bach's Gigue. Gould's gestures begin to take on a new magnitude.

INT. DAY. BOOTH.

The engineer is trying to read the paper while stretching his neck and kneading his shoulder. The assistant engineer returns, hands the producer a cup of coffee and keeps one for himself.

ASSISTANT ENGINEER
I really shouldn't be giving this to you, y'know. It's not
very good for you.

PRODUCER
You mean coffee in general or your coffee?

ASSISTANT ENGINEER
No, no, coffee and cream as a combination. It's very
bad for you. It's dangerous.

PRODUCER
Where did you get this?

INT. DAY. STUDIO.

Gould is now moving around the studio, gesturing extravagantly: he
seems almost to be in a trance.

INT. DAY. BOOTH.

ASSISTANT ENGINEER
It just sits in your stomach like ... like asphalt. I read
it in a magazine.

PRODUCER
The coffee from that machine is gonna kill me any-
ways so ... a little cream ... [to the engineer] Yeah,
you're one to talk. I mean, look at you. You're falling
apart over there. He could use some coffee.

ASSISTANT ENGINEER
Sugar, on the other hand, is actually a very good
combination. It ... it actually helps the coffee do what
it's suppose to do. So ...

71

INT. DAY. STUDIO.

Now Gould is dancing, swept away by the force of the piece. He moves as if an orchestra were watching him and he could somehow influence the music he is hearing.

INT. DAY. BOOTH.

The assistant engineer is giving the engineer a shoulder rub. The producer is finally drinking his coffee. The assistant starts playing the engineer's back with his fingertips.

                    ASSISTANT ENGINEER
          The Italian Concerto. Dum-dum-da-dum.

                         PRODUCER
          You know, this is really good. I think we have some-
          thing there.

The assistant ends the massage and everyone listens to the music. The producer looks out at Gould. They listen.

INT. DAY. STUDIO.

In counterpoint to the insistent rhythm of the music, the image of Gould's dance is gradually slowed down—giving it a new, heavy quality. After the music ends, a long silence prolongs the dance even further, and then the voice of the producer is heard once again.

                         PRODUCER
          Glenn? How's that?

                           G.G.
          There's something in that. Let's hear it again.

We hear the tape reel starting to rewind. Gould returns to sit at the piano.

OPUS 1

a composition by Glenn Gould

INT. DAY. THEATRE STAGE.

The four members of The Bruno Monsaingeon quartet sit facing each other. They play through the first movement of Glenn Gould's *Opus #1*, a little-known composition. As the romantic music sets in, we begin to move around the players in a slow graceful circle. Barely revealing its features, the theatre remains dark in the background.

The music ends, and the quartet members rise and leave the stage.

CROSSED PATHS

INT. DAY. A LIVING ROOM.

We recognize the living room from *Forty-Five Seconds and a Chair.* Strauss's Adagio from *Sonata in B minor Op. 5* begins to play and continues until the end of the sequence. A variety of characters are being interviewed, and each in turn appears sitting in Glenn Gould's chair. The camera remains fixed on this familiar tableau, content to study the variety of individuals—each of whom, by their presence, makes the scene uniquely their own.

MEGAN SMITH

I became Glenn Gould's chambermaid because the other chambermaids, who were mostly middle-aged, Italian and Jamaican women, were terrified of him. They thought he was strange, probably some sort of sexually deviant. They just found him peculiar because he was very eccentric.

WALTER HOMBURGER

When we were in Moscow in 1957, we stayed at the Canadian embassy and after the first concert, we went back into our limousine which had been loaned to us by the embassy and at the end of the concert, Glenn had received a tremendous number of flowers and big pots of mums and other flowers and as we got into the limousine, and sat down. All the flowers had been piled up there and we had barely room to sit there and Glenn said to me: 'You know Walter, it feels like we are driving to our own funeral at this point.'

RAY ROBERTS

This was his ... his passion. He really, really wanted to start, you know, retire away to Manitoulin Island, to buy a big hunk of it and bring every unwanted animal in the world there.

MEGAN SMITH

And there were numerous boxes, I think one time I counted a dozen boxes of Arrowroot cookies, sort of scattered about the room. And there were also numerous bottles of ketchup.

BOB PHILLIPS

It was a very penetrating interview, the most intelligent questions I think I'd ever heard about the North from experts, laymen or anything else, questions that required rather long answers. And as I would start to speak, or make a point, he would register his feelings not by voice but by a smile but all the time he was using his hands and conducting. And this was perhaps slightly off-putting when you're trying to think deep thoughts but, because I had no idea of what this was all about, but he continuously was just waving his arm, then sort of bring up this idea and so on. I was his orchestra for that hour.

WALTER HOMBURGER

So he decided to wear this business suit and I discussed it with him and I said: 'You know Glenn, I'm not sure that the public will understand what you're trying to convey but if you want to do it, go ahead,' which he did and he was probably the first artist that went out on stage without the, what was considered then, the proper concert attire but he again was in the forefront of change.

JILL R. COBB

He used to wake up at about 4 o'clock in the afternoon and to get himself awake, he used to phone people and I was one of those people that he phoned and, he'd talk about anything you know, he just wanted a listening board.

BOB SILVERMAN

One night he called and he was babbling on and it was probably about 1 o'clock in the morning, something like that and he ... and I fell asleep. As a matter of fact before I fell asleep, I had stretched out on the rug and I had the phone there 'cause I had been sitting in a chair and I got tired of sitting in the chair and I stretched out and he was talking, talking, talking and I wasn't talking at all and I fell asleep. And the next thing I knew, my son had walked into the room and he kick ... he was kicking me on the soles of my feet and he said: 'Wake up, there's somebody on the phone' and it was Glenn and he was talking away and I don't know how long I'd been sleeping but I didn't even remember the sequence, he was just ... the words were just pouring out.

ELYSE MACH

The phone rang and, as I picked it up, it was Glenn Gould on the other end and he said: 'Hi, this is Glenn Gould and I feel like talking.'

MARIO PRIZAK

'Mario,' he said, 'I came across the most marvellous opera for your program.'

I said, 'What is it?'

He says 'You know Ernst Krenck.'

I said, 'Yes, certainly.'

He says, 'I've got this marvellous opera by him,' he says, 'wait, I've got the score here, I'll sing it to you.'

So he sang this entire one-act opera, one-act

two-scene opera over the telephone in his not very pleasant voice.

JILL R. COBB

He was very much involved with himself, you know he didn't think of what others had to ... what others had to do or their responsibilities, you know he was consumed with what he was doing and his own things.

VALERIE VERITY

His will was that he left half of his estate to the SPCA, Society for the Prevention of Cruelties to Animals, and the other half to the Salvation Army.

VERN EDQUIST

Yes, getting 318 back from Ottawa to tune for the Conservatory when I was phoned up about it, I thought, Should I do this, I thought, No I'm going to do it just for old time sake, and when I got working on 318 again and cleaned it up and tuned it and worked on the action a bit, it felt good. So I guess I miss him. I miss his intelligent comments and I miss listening to his 20 questions not particularly to me but he was, I'll tell you one thing, today I had a customer phone me up and say: 'Can you come tomorrow to tune my piano?' Glenn Gould used to give me two- or three-months' notice and I respected that and I'm very thankful for knowing him.

TRUCK STOP

EXT. DAY. A HIGHWAY/TORONTO.

Long Fellow, Glenn Gould's Lincoln Continental, speeds along the highway. In the distance, we see the buildings of a Toronto suburb. On the far side of the road we see a sign announcing: Toronto, 20 miles. The sound of radio static mixes with the whistling of the wind and the purr of the motor: Gould is driving and tuning the car radio. The radio moves between stations, finally coming to rest on *Downtown,* performed by Petula Clark. Gould turns the volume up to maximum.

EXT. DAY. A HIGHWAY EXIT.

As Clark sings, we follow Gould's Lincoln Continental as it takes an exit off the highway and enters a truck-stop. Long Fellow eases slowly between the giant trucks in the parking lot.

INT. DAY. THE VOYAGER RESTAURANT.

Downtown, now on the restaurant radio, is heard briefy and then fades. It is lunch time in the restaurant, and there are only a few empty tables. Gould sits down at one of them. In an effort to preserve his anonymity, he leaves on his coat, his hat and his dark sunglasses. Nevertheless, the waitress is still able to catch his eye. She gives him a familiar nod, and soon she is standing before him.

85

WAITRESS
Hello Mr. Gould. Do you want the usual?

G.G.
[*politely*]
Yes, if you would be so kind.

The waitress returns behind the counter.

The atmosphere in the restaurant is calm but full of voices. A dozen simultaneous conversations create a low rumble in the room. A single voice cuts through this mass of voices and Gould turns to look. At another table, three truckers—one about fifty, the others younger—are sitting across from one another. We focus on this conversation, and soon the rumble of voices dies away artificially so that we can hear more clearly.

TRUCKER #1
Yeah, I agree ... for instance, one time up by the Reptile House, you know where that is, near Parry Sound, I see this hippy-yippy type thumbin' a ride. Long hair out to here. Figure I'll pick him up anyway, keep me entertained for a while, 'cause I'm going all night. Keep me awake. Only when I pick him up, it turns out it wasn't a hippy at all, it was a girl, a young girl. And I mean pretty like you never seen. So I says to her, 'What the hell are you doin' out here all by yourself, eh?' And a hundred miles down the road, I got her whole life story ... Seems like ... she had a fight with her boyfriend. They broke up. And she had a fight with her parents and decided to run away from home ...

Gould's attention is drawn to the beleaguered waitress at the counter. She is calculating bills and trying to deal with a troublesome but harmless regular sitting next to her. Their voices are superimposed onto the first trucker's, and are often heard simultaneously. This blend of voices begins to form a rhythmic, contrapuntal pattern.

86

TRUCKER #2

Janet.

TRUCKER #1

... generation gap or what the hell it was ...

TRUCKER #2

Janet, viens t'asseoir. J'sais que c'est pas le moment, mais il faut que j'te parle.

TRUCKER #1

A hundred miles later, she's curled up next to me ...

TRUCKER #2

Ils vont me changer ma route. J'passerai plus par Toronto. J'passerai plus par ici.

TRUCKER #1

... sweet little 16 years old thing ...

TRUCKER #2

Trois ans sur la même route c'est quand même pas pire ... Sais-tu combien de fois j'suis venu ici? J'les ai compté. Avec aujourd'hui ça fait 156 fois.

TRUCKER #1

... and you know what I did, I turned my rig around and I took her straight home, right to her house, right to the front door.

Janet dismisses Trucker #1 with a gesture of her hand.

JANET

So.

TRUCKER #1

You should have seen her parents' face.

Gould leaves this conversation before it ends and turns to face two

older truckers who are playing pool. We slowly move towards them.
Their conversation is also added to the oddly musical blend of voices
in the room. We see the small gestures of Gould's hands playing across
the top of his table as if he were conducting this 'vocal symphony'.

> TRUCKER #3
>
> Fifty bucks, I'll pay you ... Yeah.

> TRUCKER #4
>
> They screwed us, man. Damn Imlach, we'd be better
> off with Clancy.

> TRUCKER #2
>
> Pourquoi tu viens jamais à Montréal?

> TRUCKER #4
>
> Allman, Henderson, Ellis: who needs 'em. If we still
> had Mahovolich!

> TRUCKER #3
>
> Yeah, but ya don't, so pay up pal!

> JANET
>
> Because it's over. I gotta go now.

She leaves to tend to her duties.

> TRUCKER #2
>
> Because it's over. I gotta go now. Because it's over. I
> gotta go now.

> TRUCKER #3
>
> So come on rack 'em up.

> TRUCKER #4
>
> You rack 'em up.

> TRUCKER #3
>
> I rack ... so, okay ... 10 bucks ... get it ...

TRUCKER #1

And I never regret it, not a minute, never ... no sir.

As the waitress comes to the table to serve Gould his meal, the sound-track returns to reality, the room rumbling with many voices. Petula Clark singing *Downtown* fades back in.

An overhead shot allows us to see Gould's meal: scrambled eggs with a side salad and a wedge of tomato. A glass of grapefruit juice is put down near the plate. The song ends.

THE IDEA OF NORTH

a radio documentary by Glenn Gould

'The Idea of North' is the first of the three programmes that comprise 'The Solitude Trilogy', Gould's master-work for radio. Produced for the Canadian Broadcasting Corporation, it was aired on December 28, 1967. Lorne Tulk, a technician at the C.B.C., was one of Gould's closest collaborators, and he helped Gould to produce almost all of his radio programmes. The imposing 'Solitude Trilogy' was born out of this particularly intense relationship to which Tulk gave the best years of his life, often working fifteen hours a day, six days a week. This film includes an excerpt from the introduction to 'The Idea of North'.

INT. DAY. CBC RADIO BOOTH.

We are in a cramped recording studio, looking down from high above. Surrounded by recording equipment, Glenn Gould is pacing around the booth. A microphone hangs suspended before him.

> LORNE TULK
> [*off-camera*]
> O.K. Glenn, I'm ready to start. Yeah ... I'll give you ... I'll give you the whole thing from the top and when we get ... I'll just hit the record button you can start. Are you all set? Here we go ... Stand by. Ready? Here we go ... 3 ... 2 ...

For a moment we hear the garbled sound of a tape being rewound at full speed. There is a pause, and then a woman's voice begins to speak.

The voice—Schroeder, a nurse—is describing her fascination with the North. Vallee's voice mixes with Schroeder's, and the two blend into an expressive counterpoint. Gould brings in a third voice, Phillips, which joins the other two. Surprisingly, each voice finds its place in the mixture, and a fragile balance holds them together. The words detach themselves, taking on new meanings; in juxtaposition they become music.

Gould knows the flow of the broadcast by heart. He moves around the radio booth, then seats himself at a table. Instinctively, as the voices tune in, with the gestures of an orchestral conductor, he underlines their minutest nuances.

SCHROEDER
[*voice*]
I was fascinated by the country as such. I flew north from Churchill to Coral Harbour on Southampton island at the end of September. Snow had begun to fall and the country was partially covered by it. Some of the lakes were frozen around at the edges, but towards the centre of the lakes you could still see the clear, clear water. And flying over this country, you could look down and see various shades of green in the water and you could see the bottom of the lakes, and it was a most fascinating experience. I remember I was up in the cockpit with the pilot, and I was forever looking out, left and right, and I could see ice-floes over the Hudson's Bay and I was always looking for a polar bear or some seals that I could spot but, unfortunately, there were none.

SCHROEDER I
And as we flew along the east coast of the Hudson's Bay, this flat, flat country
VALLEE 2
[*voice*]
I don't go, let me say

S I
frightened me a little because it just seemed endless.
V2
this again, I don't go for this northmanship bit at all.

S I
We seemed to be going into nowhere, and the further north we
V2
I don't know those people who do claim they want to go

94

S I

went the more monotonous it became. There was

V 2

farther and farther north, but I see it as a game—this

S I

nothing but snow and, to our right, the waters of

V 2

northmanship bit. People say, 'Well were you ever up at the

S I

Hudson's Bay.——— Now this was my impression

V 2

North Pole?' and, 'Hell I did a dog-sled trip of twenty-
two days'

S I

during the winter, but I also flew over the country

V 2

and the other fellow says, 'Well I did one of thirty days.'

S I

during the spring and the summer, and this I found

V 2

You know, it's pretty childish. Perhaps they would see

PHILIPS 3

[*voice*]

And then for another 11 years, I served the North in

S I

intriguing; because, then, I could see the outlines

V 2

themselves as more sceptical———[fade]

P 3

various capacities. Sure the North has changed my
life; I can't

S I

of the lakes and the rivers and, on the tundra,

Production stills from *Thirty-Two Short Films About Glenn Gould*. Colm Feore as GLENN GOULD.

1. *Forty-Five Seconds and a Chair*
2, 3. *Gould Meets Gould*
4. *The L.A. Concert*
5, 6. *Passion According to Gould*
7. *Truck Stop*
8. *The Idea of North*
9, 10. *The Tip* (with Jimmy Loftus as WAITER #1 and Frank Canino as WAITER #2)
11. *Personal Ad*
12. *Forty-Nine*
13. *Motel Wawa*

Photos: Cylla von Tiedemann.

conceive of anyone being in close touch with the
North

S I

huge spots of moss

P 3

whether they lived there all the time or simply
travelled it

S I

or rock—there is hardly any

V 2

more skeptical about

P 3

month after month and year after year—I can't
conceive of such

S I

vegetation that one can spot from the air———[*fade*]

V 2

about the offerings of the mass media———[fade]

P 3

a person as really being untouched by the North.

V 2

And it goes on like

P 3

When I left in 1965, at least, left the job there, it
wasn't because

V 2

this, as though there's some special merit, some virtue, in
being

P 3

of being tired of the North, the feeling that it had
no more

V2

in the North, or some special virtue in having been with

P3

interest, or anything of the sort; I was keen as ever. I
left

V2

*primitive people: well, you know, what special virtue is
there*

P3

because I'm a public servant, [*begin fade*] I was asked
to do ...

The camera slowly descends to Gould's level, and by the time it reaches him, he is almost immobile, content to listen to the continuing flow
of voices. After a time, the voices fade away and the red glow from an
'On Air' light bathes the small room. Gould pulls the microphone
towards himself.

G.G.

This is Glenn Gould, and this program is called 'The
Idea of North'.

SOLITUDE

Solitude contains excerpts from an interview that Glenn Gould gave to Jonathan Cott of Rolling Stone magazine *(Vol. 167, August 15, 1974, pp. 38 to 46)*.

EXT. DAY. THE FAR NORTH.

The frame is filled with impenetrable whiteness, an image recalling the opening sequence. Over this whiteness we hear the voice of an interviewer, Jonathan Cott, calling across from a distance.

> COTT
> Let's talk about the radio documentaries you made for the C.B.C. [*Sibelius' Andantino from* Sonata #2 *begins to play*] Two of your programmes: 'The Idea of North' and 'The Latecomers', are both about the idea of solitude as it affects people living in Northern Canada.

Glenn Gould moves slowly into frame. We follow him as he paces, then turns to face the invisible interviewer.

> G.G.
> In fact all those programmes deal to some degree with solitude. There are five programmes I've made that have taken three or four hundred hours of studio time. Number one was, as you mentioned, 'The Idea of North', two was 'The Latecomers', three was 'Stokowski', four is one we're just mixing now on Casals ... 'Casals: A Portrait for Radio'. I'm doing one next year on Schoenberg, and there's one that's lain around now for a year and a half. It's a programme on the Mennonites called 'Quiet in the Land', and that is

the ultimate in community isolation. So next I want
to do a comedy about an isolated man, because I'm
sick and tired of all these profound statements.

COTT

Well, radio itself is a solitary experience. Why does it
interest you as a medium?

G.G.

I'd like to deal with this as sensibly as I can, it's a big
question, it's an important question. I don't know what
the effective ratio would be but I've always had some
sort of intuition that for every hour you spend with
other human beings you need X number of hours
alone. Now what that ... X represents I don't really
know whether it be two and seven-eighths or seven
and two-eighths, but it's a substantial ratio. Radio is
something that's always been very close to me ever
since I was a child, sometimes I listen to it virtually
non-stop: I mean it's wallpaper for me. I sleep with the
radio on, in fact now I'm incapable of sleeping without the radio on, ever since I gave up Nembutal.

COTT

Does it affect your dreams?

The camera moves in to a close-up on Gould.

G.G

Sure, in so far as if there is a broadcast on the hour, I
will pick up the bulletins and dream them and, in the
morning, if there's been a boat that's just gone down
I'll think, Gee, that was an odd dream about the
Titanic I had last night. And I will have, of course,
gone through it.

COTT

Maybe your feelings of solitude come from your

Nordic temperament.

I think that's certainly part of it. It's always been an ambition of mine, which I'll probably never get around to realizing, to spend at least one winter north of the Arctic Circle. Anyone can go there in the summer when the sun is up, I want to go there when the sun is down, I really do, and so help me I'm going to do it one of these times. I've being saying this for five or six years now and every year the schedule gets in the way.

COTT

Well, I hope you do. Thank you very much Mr. Gould.

The music ends. Gould walks away.

QUESTIONS WITH NO ANSWERS

EXT. DAY. PHONE BOOTH OUTSIDE TORONTO CITY HALL.

The Prelude from Bach's *English Suite #2* begins to play. A music critic is standing in a phone booth. He is speaking on the telephone, and barely managing to hold onto the paper on which he is clumsily taking notes.

> CRITIC
>
> Mr. Gould, thank you for the interview yesterday. I would just like some further clarifications if I may ... Good ... Where am I? ... Okay here we are. ... Now if it's really true that you attach little importance to the actual technique of playing the piano, how is it you have managed to obtain such a level of skill at it.? Well that is to say, don't you think it's depressing for all the young pianists in the world to know this.

INT. DAY. A MAGAZINE OFFICE.

A stylish journalist, a little bit older than she would like us to think, is sitting on the sofa in her mod office. The room is occasionally lit by the popping flashbulbs of the photographer who accompanies her. The journalist looks directly into the camera and, with a cocky air of self-assurance, begins the interview.

> JOURNALIST
> Glenn Gould, Glenn Gould, Glenn Gould ... Glenn

Gould, I really want to thank you from the bottom of my heart for arranging for me to have this chance to interview you finally and before we begin the interview, I also want to give you a great big thank you on behalf of all our readers.

INT. DAY. A WRITER'S HOME OFFICE.

In the half-light of a room that is full of books, a writer is sitting at his desk, speaking on the telephone. He speaks in tones that are both scholarly and friendly.

> WRITER
>
> These are tough questions, they are going to come up, people are going to watch the play, they're going to ask me ... Glenn Gould is apparently incredibly interested in technology but, really, wasn't technology just a reason or a way for him to keep the world at arm's length? It's just a big smoke-screen, isn't it?

INT. DAY. MAGAZINE OFFICE.

> JOURNALIST
>
> Let me ask you this. What is Glenn Gould really like when he's not in a studio? I mean what do ya like to do when you're outside of the recording booth? What kind of lifestyle do you lead?

The reporter waits expectantly for a response.

EXT. DAY. PHONE BOOTH.

> CRITIC
>
> Mr. Gould, you are a perfectionist when it comes to recording. So why is it that when you are recording you place little importance on whether you have a

piano with noisy works, or a chair that squeaks? Why, when you seem obsessed with this idea of musical perfection, do you hum as you play?

INT. DAY. A DRESSING ROOM.

A twelve-year-old girl stands near to a piano, and her proud mother sits near to her. The girl looks into the camera as her mother encourages her daughter to speak. The girl turns back towards her mother.

> YOUNG GIRL
> Well ... ummm ... I forgot the question.

INT. DAY. MAGAZINE OFFICE.

> JOURNALIST
> I mean what aspects of your life has nothing to do with ... with, with ... anything that has to do with classical, musical ... music.

INT. NIGHT. WRITER'S HOME OFFICE.

The writer is sitting at his desk, still speaking on the phone.

> WRITER
> Years ago you said that you were going to leave the public performance because you wanted to compose, and we've waited and years have passed and there's no body of work, I mean musically speaking and ... people are waiting ... how do you feel about all that?

INT. DAY. DRESSING ROOM.

The young girl tries another sortie. At first she stammers and then finally spits out the question.

YOUNG GIRL
Would … Would you teach me the piano?

She stands, almost breathless with anticipation, waiting for an answer
that never comes.

INT. DAY. MAGAZINE OFFICE.

At the outset there is a long silence. The journalist finally rallies herself
and pushes on with the interview.

JOURNALIST
What about children? I mean, have you thought
about that? What do you look for in a woman? Or
maybe I should say, what are you waiting for?

EXT. DAY. PHONE BOOTH.

CRITIC
One more question, if I may, out of curiosity. Why do
you insist on conducting interviews by phone?

INT. NIGHT. UNIVERSITY AUDITORIUM.

A woman of about forty sits on a desk. She addresses the camera con-
fidently, speaking in French. Sitting next to her we see a translator
desperately trying to follow her convoluted question.

PROFESSOR
Monsieur Gould, vous avez affirmé qu'il y a dans
notre culture des forces économiques et sociales qui
sont à l'oeuvre et qui ont déjà rendu caduques les
salles de concert. Vous, vous anticipiez d'ailleurs la dis-
parition de ces salles autour de l'an 2000. En quoi cet
énoncé permet-il de jeter un nouveau regard sur la
mécanique et l'économie du marché musical et sur

l'asservissement de l'artiste à ce système?

SUBTITLE: You've said that economic and social forces have rendered concert halls obsolete. They will disappear by the year 2000. What does this say about the workings and economy of the music market and the artist's subjugation to it?

> TRANSLATOR

Well ... umm ... Caduques.

INT. NIGHT. WRITER'S HOME OFFICE.

> WRITER

I know, now the concerts can't go on, it's been talked about, it's been explained, all the reasons but ... when you think about it. On the day that it happened ... it was about fear wasn't it?

INT. NIGHT. UNIVERSITY AUDITORIUM.

> PROFESSOR

Enfin alors que vous concevez ce nouvel ordre culturel comme un affranchissement de l'artiste, il apparaît plutôt de mon point de vue que cette vision encourage une techno-hégémonie et l'exploitation de l'artiste par des méga-structures capitalistes, non?

SUBTITLE: While you believe this new cultural order will liberate the artist, won't this vision encourage a techno-hegemony and the artist's exploitation by capitalist mega-stuctures?

INT. DAY. MAGAZINE OFFICE.

> JOURNALIST

I've asked you about your music, I've asked you about your family, I've asked you about your children, I've asked you what you have for dinner, I've asked you what you do when you go to a movie.

INT. NIGHT. UNIVERSITY AUDITORIUM.

The professor looks intently at the translator. We see the translator trying to pull himself together before tackling the question. He pauses to take a breath before beginning.

> TRANSLATOR
> Mr. Gould ... You've stated that the concert hall is becoming more and more of an economic liability, but that you foresee this problem rectifying itself by the year 2000. Why?

INT. DAY. MAGAZINE OFFICE.

The journalist has completely lost her poise and confidence. The photographer leaves the office. She lights a cigarette, pulls herself together and continues the interview.

> JOURNALIST
> O.K. Fine. Are you homosexual?

The music ends.

INT. NIGHT. HOTEL ROOM/DOWNTOWN IN A LARGE CITY.

The room is dark. A woman stands with her back to a window that offers a view of downtown. She is speaking on the telephone. The camera moves slowly towards her.

> WOMAN
> Glenn, why didn't you answer my calls? Why did you stop calling me?

A LETTER

CLOSE ON: LETTER.

As the camera passes over a letter, written on blue-lined paper with a black felt pen, Bach's Variation #19 from *The Goldberg Variations* begins to play. Gould reads his words.

> G.G.
>
> [*voice-over*]
>
> *You know, I am deeply in love with a certain beautiful girl. I asked her to marry me but she turned me down but I still love her more than anything in the world and every minute I can spend with her is pure heaven. But I don't want to be a bore and if I can only get her to tell me when I could see her, it would help. She has a standing invitation to let me take her anywhere she'd like to go, anytime, but it seems to me she never has time for me. Please if you see her, ask her to let me know when I can see her, and when I can—*

Gould's handwriting breaks off mid-sentence. The music ends.

GOULD MEETS McLAREN

animation by Norman McLaren

In 1969, Norman McLaren created three short animations, called Spheres, *for inclusion in 'The Well-Tempered Listener', a programme created and produced by Glenn Gould. These animated films bear witness to the intellectual kinship and the aesthetic similarities of these two great Canadian artists. The third of these short films is presented, in its entirety, in* Gould Meets McLaren.

ANIMATION.

Excerpt from *Spheres* by Norman McLaren and René Jodoin, National Film Board of Canada.

A white sphere, textured by light, slowly descends to the centre of the screen. On the first note of Bach's Fugue #14 from *The Well-Tempered Clavier,* the sphere divides in perfect synchronization. The two new spheres move away from each other in opposite directions and, upon reaching the edge of frame, they divide again. Four spheres now separate, divide, and then divide again.

The movements of these spheres begin to form a ballet that marries perfectly with the music, taking full advantage of the dynamics of depth and perspective. As in Bach's music, the structure of the work becomes less perceivable, reflecting more and more the unique skill of the artist.

In a gesture of recapitulation the spheres begin a series of different, symmetrical movements, fusing together until they have once again formed the single sphere seen at the outset. In the background, a nebulous cloud shifts and folds in on itself. The music ends.

THE TIP

Prokofiev's Precipitato from *Sonata #7* begins to play. The pacing of this film is relentlessly verbal, mirroring the frenetic nature of the stock exchange and its clipped, neologistic language.

STOCK FOOTAGE.

A sheik being met at the airport by various officials. They move through the airport. Then, footage of oil-rig drilling. We hear the voice of a TV announcer.

> TV ANNOUNCER
> [*off-camera*]
> Sheik Ahmed Zaki Yamani arrived in Ottawa today to begin a series of discussions across Canada about the future of oil prices. The powerful Gandi Oil Minister will meet tomorrow with …

INT. DAY. A BROKERAGE OFFICE.

We move through the ranks of a busy brokerage firm in full swing, a portrait gallery of frenzied personnel—receiving orders from clients, calling orders to the floor. Angry, tired and sweaty functional alcoholics with bad ties, nicotine stains and pointy collars or rolled-up shirtsleeves; whatever their position in the hierarchy, everyone is on the phone.

In other words, all is well. The market is bullish and clients are buy-ing, buying, buying. A hot-shot young broker studies the ticker tape and rattles along eagerly and cheerfully to his client on the other end of the line.

BROKER #1

Howie, thanks for holding. It's me, your fairy god-mother. Y'just cleared 30 Grand in your sleep.

A second, older and gruffer broker is also busily talking on the phone.

BROKER #2

12,000 Texas Gulf at 46. Call me and let me know how the options open. [*he picks up another line*] Sorry sir, what's on the recommender? Play it safe. I'm stick-ing with the big one, oil that is ... Black gold ... Texas tea.

BROKER #1

Across the board: Gulf, Dome, Petrofina, take your pick and hold on the ride. We're going through the roof here. I'm looking at 32 by the bell ... Okay.

INT. DAY. PHILLIP BRENNAN'S OFFICE.

We end up in Phillip Brennan's modest office. The desk is framed by a window, from ceiling to floor, that offers an impressive, if not cluttered, view looking down into the city's core.

Brennan is sitting behind the desk, smoking a cigarette and talking on the phone to an obstinate client.

BRENNAN

... Sotex Resources? No never heard of it. Yeah, I'll check the charts ...

He spins around, grabs a binder and flips it open.

BRENNAN

Yeah, but again, I'm telling you, oil right now is as
close to a sure thing as we got in this business. It's
crazy to sell. Sotex ... No ... Got nothing on it.
Sounds risky to me but you want it, you got it.

The frame opens wider and we see that there is another man in the
room. He is sitting in the chair across from the desk, drinking a cup of
coffee. Desmond is elegant and conspicuously wealthy.

DESMOND
[pointing to Brennan's phone]
Who's that? Who is it?

Brennan covers the phone with his hand and answers under his breath.

BRENNAN

Glenn Gould. [to the phone] I'll just ask you to remember in the days and weeks ahead that this was your
bright idea ... That's my job. Later.

He hangs up the phone and starts to dial another number.

DESMOND
[laughing slightly]
The piano player?

BRENNAN

Yeah, Glenn Gould the piano player. [on the phone]
Okay, got a buy for you, 10,000 STX, Gould.

Desmond sips from his cup.

INT. DAY. ROYAL YORK HOTEL RESTAURANT.

Glenn Gould, at his regular table, is talking about the day's trade with
the elderly waiter. A second waiter sets a table nearby.

125

G.G.

What is the special of the day?

WAITER #1

Canstar Oil and Gas.

G.G..

Eleven and three quarters.

WAITER #1

Mr. Mackie had lunch with the minister. There's an incentive program in the air.

G.G.

Well, I don't buy it.

WAITER #1

He's in for ninety-thou.

The second waiter comes to clear the table.

WAITER #1

The Pormack brothers are in tight with the Saudis ... they've been mopping it up all week.

WAITER #2

So as long as this embargo holds ...

WAITER #1

[mimicking the song]
It's going up, up and away ...

WAITER #2

Anything else Mr. Gould?

G.G.

Yes. I'll have a cup of coffee and a telephone.

The second waiter leaves.

WAITER #1

Everybody's buying.

G.G.

Well I'm afraid I can't agree.

WAITER #1

What do you mean? Do you know something?

G.G.

I had a small word with Sheik Yamani's bodyguard at
the airport and, uh ...

The waiter leans down close to Gould.

WAITER #1

And what ...?

Gould scans through the business section and circles a stock in the listings.

G.G.

Now, this one has to be kept strictly between you and me.

Gould rips the marked section out of the paper and hands it to the waiter.

WAITER #1

STX ... Sotex Resources? Never heard of it.

G.G.

The Sheik has, and he's about to deliver them a major
explorations contract.

The waiter stuffs the paper in his breast pocket. The second waiter
comes, puts the phone on the table and leaves.

INSERT.

The newspaper stock listing, showing Sotex at 5 1/4.

INT. DAY. ROYAL YORK HOTEL RESTAURANT.

The waiter walks away. When he's out of sight, he pulls the paper from his pocket and looks at it with raised eyebrows. He shows it to the second waiter who is coming with the coffee. Gould is watching. He smiles quietly, picks up the receiver of the table phone and dials.

> G.G.
> [*on the phone*]
> This is entirely entre-nous, this is just between you and me.

INSERT.

The newspaper stock listing, showing Sotex at 6 7/8.

INT. DAY. A DESK.

From above we see a woman on the phone, consulting a newspaper listing. We hear a voice.

> VOICE #1
> Sotex ... Hang on one sec ... here it is.

INSERT.

The newspaper stock listing, showing Sotex at 7 7/8.

INT. DAY. ROYAL YORK HOTEL RESTAURANT.

The waiter gives the paper to a businessman at the bar. The businessman slips the waiter a couple of bills.

> WAITER #1
> A little stock called Sotex. Ever heard of it?

INSERT.

The newspaper stock listing, showing Sotex at 10 1/4.

INT. DAY. ROYAL YORK HOTEL RESTAURANT.

The first waiter, tray in hand, whispers to a businessman.

INT. DAY. ANOTHER DESK.

A hand scribbles on a sheet of paper. Again we hear someone on the phone.

> VOICE #2
> Sotex ten and a third, get me twenty thousand shares.

INT. DAY. ROYAL YORK HOTEL RESTAURANT.

Behind the bar, the second waiter whispers over the telephone.

> WAITER #2
> Mines, natural resources, stuff from up North, you
> know. Listen, Sheik Romani is very interested in this
> company ...

STOCK FOOTAGE.

A newspaper spins into view. The headline reads: THE LITTLE STOCK THAT
COULD. Footage of oil rigs. Then, the floor of the stock exchange: a flurry of shouting and gesticulating.

INSERT.

The newspaper stock listing, showing Sotex at 13.

STOCK FOOTAGE.

The exchange floor and the stock index. The floor closes. Traders on the floor throw their chits in the air. We hear the voice of a TV announcer.

> TV ANNOUNCER
> [*off-camera*]
> The TSE dropped 40 points as a result of this morning's announcement and the Dow fell back an alarming 72 points. One of the few bright spots in the midst of this doom and gloom was a tiny company called Sotex Resources which closed at 15.3.

INSERT.

A newspaper spins up close and stops. It is *The Globe and Mail* and the headline reads: BAD DAY FOR STOCKS. Another headline, from *Le Devoir*, reads: JOURNÉE NOIRE AUX BOURSES CANADIEN.

INT. DAY/LATER THAT WEEK. BROKERAGE OFFICE.

We follow the same route as our last visit. This time tensions are high— phones are slammed down, clients are irate. We see Broker #2 on the phone.

> BROKER #2
> Ten and a quarter! Well ditch it for Christ's sake. What are you waiting for?

We see Broker #1, also on the phone.

> BROKER #1
> Yeah, Howie ... unfortunately we are looking at a bit of a dip ... down 12 points ... well, that's the way the game works. You know the risk. Sotex? Sure. ... You want a piece?

BROKER #2
[*on the phone*]
Yeah, look sir. What do you want me to say? You lost,
I lost, everybody lost ... take it up with OPEC.

He hangs up and starts to dial another number. The music ends.

INT. DAY. BRENNAN'S OFFICE.

Brennan is on the blower, as usual, seated behind his desk.

BRENNAN
Whatever you say, Glenn. You know, I have to confess,
you were my only client who made a buck last week.
And a pretty good one too ... Hey, listen, you gave up
touring. Maybe you should give up playing the piano
altogether and just play the market. That's right, a vir-
tuoso. Yeah, I'll talk to you soon ...

He hangs up the phone and mutters to himself.

BRENNAN
A piano player.

PERSONAL AD

The text of Personal Ad *was found in Gould's papers.*

INT. NIGHT. GLENN GOULD'S STUDY/TORONTO.

We find the book- and paper-cluttered interior of Glenn Gould's study at his Inn On The Park apartment—an area that seems to defy the laws of physics by the amount of papers, books and assorted bits of technical equipment that have been crammed into its small space.

As Scriabin's Désir from *Two Pieces Op. 57* begins to play, the camera travels over this debris and we hear the sound of a typewriter. We finally come to rest on Glenn Gould as he types a few final words and then pulls a piece of paper from his typewriter.

At first he remains seated, his lips barely moving as he re-reads what he has just written. After a moment he rises and begins to walk through the confining space of his study.

A series of jump cuts, close-ups and high overhead shots show us Gould as he rehearses the delivery of his personal advertisement.

G.G.

Wanted.
    Friendly, companionably reclusive, socially unacceptable, alcoholically abstemious, tirelessly talkative, zealously unzealous, spiritually intense, minimally turquoise, maximally ecstatic loon seeks moth or moths with similar equalities for purposes of telephonic seduction, Tristan-esque trip-taking ...

tristan-esque, tristan-esque trip-taking, and perma-
nent flame-fluttering. No photos required. Financial
status immaterial. All ages and non-competitive voca-
tions considered. Applicants should furnish cassettes
of sample conversation, notarized certification of
marital dis-inclination, references re low-decibel
vocal consistency, itinerary and … itinerary and sample receipts from previous, successfully completed
out-of-town moth flights. All submissions treated
confidentially. No paws need apply. The auditions for
all promising candidates will be conducted to and on
Anaton Penisend, Newfoundland.

At times he pauses and relishes a particular phrase—repeating it three
or four times before continuing—while at others he rushes through the
text—feeling out its subtle rhythms rather than examining the words
themselves. Occasionally we see Gould pause to make a small correc-
tion. Finally satisfied, he moves to the phone and begins to dial as the
music ends.

OPERATOR
[*off-camera*]
Toronto Star Classified, good afternoon.

Gould listens to the operator, then hangs up the phone without speaking.

PILLS

The Sehr Lebhaft from Hindemith's *Sonata #3* begins to play. As we examine the various textures, shapes and colours of the arsenal of pills that Glenn Gould used to treat a host of real and imaginary ailments, we hear Gould's voice as he impassively reads off the uses and effects of these pills.

INSERT.

Extreme close-up of white pills.

G.G.

[*voice-over*]

Valium. A minor tranquilizer used to relieve symptoms of tension and anxiety. Avoid using this medication in conjunction with antidepressants ...

INSERT.

Extreme close-up of a pile of blue pills.

[*voice-over*]

Trifluoperazine. An anti-psychotic prescribed for moderate to severe depression and anxiety. This medication may cause an inability to sleep. Do not take in conjunction with barbiturates ...

INSERT.

Extreme close-up of orange capsules.

> [*voice-over*]
> *Like other barbiturates, Pentobarbital acts by interfering with nerve impulses to the brain. Long-term use may result in addiction. Side-effects include drowsiness, lethargy and a general allergic reaction …*

INSERT.

Extreme close-up of a small pile of green capsules.

> [*voice-over*]
> *Librax is most commonly used to soothe the anxiety often associated with gastrointestinal disorders. The effects of Librax may be inhibited by certain medications used in the treatment of high blood-pressure …*

INSERT.

Extreme close-up of a single orange pill.

> [*voice-over*]
> *Aldomet is used to control high blood-pressure. A mild sedative effect or transient headache are possible side-effects … Aldomet will increase the effectiveness of other anti-hypertensives …*

INSERT.

Extreme close-up of an array of white pills.

> [*voice-over*]
> *Clonidine acts in the brain by causing the dilation of certain*

blood vessels. Side-effects include drowsiness, dizziness, headache and fatigue ...

INSERT.

Extreme close-up of a small blue-and-pink capsule.

> [*voice-over*]
> *Indocin, a non-steroidal agent used to treat various forms of joint and muscle inflammation. It can produce severe stomach upset, rashes, itching and even a ringing in the ears ...*

INSERT.

Extreme close-up of a pile of orange pills.

> [*voice-over*]
> *Hydrochlorothiazide, an anti-hypertensive used in the treatment of high blood-pressure. Side-effects include headache, restlessness and a depressed sex drive ...*

INSERT.

Extreme close-up of a pile of white pills.

> [*voice-over*]
> *Septra, an anti-infective used to treat infections of the urinary tract ... may cause itching, rashes, drug-fever or arthritis-like pain ...*

INSERT.

Extreme close-up of blue-and-white capsules.

141

[voice-over]
*Fiorinal, a non-narcotic pain reliever ... can lead to drug
dependence or addiction ... interaction with Phenylbutazone
may cause stomach irritation ...*

INSERT.

Extreme close-up of a pile of small red pills.

[voice-over]
*Phenylbutazone. An anti-inflammatory often used to treat
pain in the shoulder due to bursitis ... prolonged use may
lead to excessive water retention ...*

INSERT.

Extreme close-up of a pile of white pills.

[voice-over]
*Chlorothiazide, a diuretic used in the treatment of high
blood-pressure or in a situation where it is necessary to rid
the body of excess water. Avoid using the conjunction with
drugs that have a stimulant effect ...*

INSERT.

Extreme close-up of orange pills.

[voice-over]
*Allopurinol, an anti-gout medication. A major side-effect is
exhaustion and a desire to sleep. Avoid tasks that require
concentration.*

The music ends.

MARGARET PACSU

friend

Margaret Pacsu is a Canadian radio host and media figure. For many years she and Glenn Gould shared an abiding friendship, and they worked together on several projects for the C.B.C.

EXT. LAKEFRONT.

We see a lake and the horizon and hear the engine of an airplane fly-ing overhead. Margaret Pacsu is sitting on a bench with her back to the lake as she talks about Glenn Gould.

> PACSU
> He didn't talk to me about drugs very much except these instances when he would excuse himself and then, it was interesting, of course there was a bath-room in this hotel suite and I asked him if I could use the bathroom, these sessions went on for six and seven hours and so I did, I remember going in there and seeing lined up on the wall all these different bottles and I came out and I said, 'Drug ...,' I said, 'Glenn, surely you're not taking all this stuff, are you?' and he said, 'Well no not all at once' and he sort of laughed. I don't understand that in him, I never understood that and he ... I didn't have the feeling that he was acting in a ... in a way that had been produced by a drug. He was neither speeding nor was he sort of, you know, not in control of his ... any kinds of anything and here was this line-up of bottles.

DIARY OF ONE DAY

Glenn Gould was particularly concerned with his state of health. So much so, that a number of specialists pronounced him to be a hypochondriac. Throughout his life, both alone and with doctors, he nurtured a daunting medical regime. This attitude of Gould's reflected not so much a phobia, but rather an extreme musical awareness of his own body. Diary of One Day *contains several extracts from Gould's 'Health Diary' in the National Library of Canada.*

A BLACK SCREEN.

CUT TO TEXT IN SUPER.
9:00 a.m., Aldomet (1) Blood pressure 140/100 (est)

INSERT. AN X-RAY MONITOR.
The Gigue from Schoenberg's *Suite for Piano Op. 25* begins to play. The image of a beating heart is seen through the medium of an X-ray monitor. We can clearly see the movement of the blood as the arteries around the heart appear to be almost transparent. The various vessels rise and fall to the rhythm of the heartbeats we hear pulsing in counterpoint to the music.

CUT TO TEXT IN SUPER.
152/112 to 160/116

CUT TO TEXT IN SUPER.
4:00 p.m., Aldomet (2)

CUT TO MONITOR.
We see the image of a beating heart. Then we see the area of the arm where it meets the elbow. Here the vessels are smaller and the flow of

blood more rare. The elbow bends and unbends in a rhythm that matches that of the music. We next see an image of the skull, facing us and also moving with the music. Finally, we return to the beating heart.

CUT TO TEXT IN SUPER.
144/112

CUT TO MONITOR.
The image on the X-ray monitor is a hand, moving as if it were playing a piano. We move to an image of the ribcage and up to the closely knit arteries of the neck.

CUT TO TEXT IN SUPER.
5:00 p.m. Gravol (3) 148/110 148/108 142/104

CUT TO MONITOR.
We see the image of a skull, from the side, nodding to the rhythm of the music.

CUT TO TEXT IN SUPER.
6:20 p.m., Valium (1)

CUT TO MONITOR.
The image in the monitor moves from the hands, playing, up to the skull, seen from the front and side, and down to the arms.

CUT TO TEXT IN SUPER.
7:00 p.m. 138/112 44/112 142/112 138/108

CUT TO TEXT IN SUPER.
7:15 p.m.

CUT TO MONITOR.
The image of the beating heart.

CUT TO TEXT IN SUPER.
7:30 p.m., 152/ 112 to 160/116

CUT TO MONITOR.
The image moves throughout the upper body, from the nodding skull down to the hands, up the vertebrae to the heart, down to a tapping foot and up to the moving elbows.

CUT TO TEXT IN SUPER.
8:00 p.m., Valium

CUT TO MONITOR.
The image of hands moving and then the beating heart. What was fore-shadowed in the previous image is now a certainty: these are the bones, veins and flowing blood of Gould as he plays the piano.

CUT TO TEXT IN SUPER.
8:30 p.m., 136/98 138/98
138/112 144/112 142/112 138/108

CUT TO MONITOR.
The beating-heart image.

CUT TO TEXT IN SUPER.
138/98 137/98

CUT TO TEXT IN SUPER.
9:00 p.m., after (O-J)

CUT TO MONITOR.

As the music dies away we return to the image of the heart, still beating in the same, inexorable rhythm. The image slowly fades.

MOTEL WAWA

Wawa is a small town on the shore of Lake Superior where Gould liked to spend time on his own, staying in a small motel that faced the water. The interview text is from Great Pianists Speak for Themselves, *Elyse Mach, Dover Publishers..*

EXT. DUSK. LAKE SUPERIOR.

Under a darkening sky, we look out from a beach over Lake Superior.

INT. DUSK. A MOTEL ROOM/WAWA.

The Ruhig bewegte Viertel from Hindemith's *Sonata #1* begins to play as we discover Glenn Gould in the middle of an interview with Elyse Mach. He sits on a chair, the telephone receiver in his hand. An open window in the centre of the frame is the only source of light in the bleak motel room. As Gould speaks, we slowly move in. He turns, stands, crosses the frame and looks out at the beach and the forbidding grey lake. We creep inexorably forward as the conversation continues.

> MACH
> Mr. Gould, we've covered a lot of the topics that I wanted to cover with you. But could we perhaps move on to some of the more personal questions? Tell me, do you believe in the supernatural? Or in ESP?

> G.G.
> You know, no one has never asked me that before. 'Do I believe in the supernatural?' Of course. Yes … and no. That is to say I don't hold to this notion that one's mind can be read like a book or some such thing. But that there are certain inexplicable coincidences in the

155

world seems, to me, patently obvious.

MACH

Have you ever experienced any one of those coincidences? Could you tell me about it?

G.G.

Yes, several times ... the oddest being when I was very young, nine years old. I should preface this by saying that I have always been fascinated by dreams, and the kind of feeling that they leave one with. There's a certain horrible ... feeling, tragic sense of loss, that one can derive only from a dream. Anyway at this time, I was about nine years old ... pardon me ... about nine years old and I had this peculiar dream, in which I saw myself covered with red spots. The next morning, when I mentioned it to my mother, she'd had exactly the same dream. Now at that time there was no hint of measles, no epidemic, no worry of any kind. So the dreams certainly can't have been affected by any external common suggestion. And yet four days later, I got the measles.

MACH

Very interesting. Tell me, continuing, what do you believe regarding afterlife?

G.G.

Well I was brought up a Presbyterian, though I stopped being a church goer, at—ohh—about the age of 18 ... I've always felt tremendously strongly that there is indeed a hereafter ... with which we must all reckon, in light of which we must live our lives and there is that inevitability of the transformation of the spirit. As a consequence, I find all 'here-and-now' philosophies quite repellent ... lax, if you will. I realize however, that there's a great temptation to formulate a comfortable theory about eternal life so as to reconcile oneself to the inevitability of death. But I'd like to think that's not what I'm doing. I don't believe I'm trying to create for myself a deliberate self-reassuring process. It just seems intuitively right. I've never had to work very hard convincing myself of a hereafter. After all, don't you think it seems infinitely more plausible than its opposite … oblivion?

The music ends, and Gould moves away from the window, which by now fills the entire frame. We look out the window on the beach and the lake.

FORTY-NINE

Forty-Nine *is based on 'Death in the Afternoon'*, Glenn Gould, Week End *magazine, Vol. 16, No. 27, 1956.*

EXT. DUSK. INDUSTRIAL ZONE/TORONTO.

Again we hear the music of Schoenberg, this time the Leicht Zart from *Six Little Pieces for Piano*. We are at the edge of a waterway, with factories and loading docks in the background. Glenn Gould's Lincoln Continental is parked near a telephone booth on the wide expanse of a vacant lot that lies beside the river. Gould is inside the booth, and we see him through its open glass door.

G.G.

[nervously]

Hello Jessie, it's me. I wonder if you, could you indulge me for a moment. I'm in a bit of a state. Well, I was driving along when I suddenly remembered that story about Schoenberg ... Schoenberg! Remember he was obsessed with numerology, numbers and so forth. So much so that when he turned 65 he was terrified that he was going to die because his age was divisible by 13. So he consulted an astrologer friend who assured him that he would survive until the next time the numbers conspired against him. Well great, he thought, another 13 years, I'll be fine until I am 78. Eleven years later, however, when he was 76, the astrologer wrote back to warn him that it's not only numbers that are divisible by 13 that he ought to watch out for, but also those whose digits add up to 13, for example 76. Needless to say he was petrified, but not for long. Three months later, he died, July 13th, 1951. I can't help it, I'm 49 tomorrow and Schoenberg's still talking to me ...

Silence.

G.G.

Jessie, Jessie, are you there?

The music ends.

JESSIE GREIG

cousin

Jessie Greig was more than just a cousin to Gould; she also took on the roles of sister, confidante and best friend. They formed a close relationship at a young age that was to last right up until the time of Gould's death.

INT. DAY. GREIG'S APARTMENT/OSHAWA.

Jessie Greig is seated by a window. Behind her the view is framed by autumn foliage.

> GREIG
> The week before he died, I remember it in great detail. And it's funny that, it's peculiar that I do remember it in such detail because many of the times our conversations were light and just banter between two good friends. But the week before Glenn died, everything was serious. He couldn't control the birthday that was coming up, the celebration. He couldn't … he … he seemed to think everything was slipping away from his control and he was obsessed with this feeling that he wondered, would people recognize him and come to a funeral and we never talked about anything like that before … but he said that he wanted … he didn't … he would like to be like Huckleberry Finn and come to his own funeral because he didn't think that there would be people who came. He didn't think that the world loved him like they did and he knew about how the records were selling, he knew that they were very … that Japanese people brought … bought a lot of them, that people … in Central Europe … and in Asia bought a lot of them but he just didn't think that he was that

165

important and it never surfaced that, to me at least, that he felt his own … fame. His humility was beyond everything. And when I saw the people pour into Saint Paul's Cathedral, I couldn't help but believe, 'Oh! Glenn, you were wrong for probably the first time in your life', you know 'cause he always liked to think he never was wrong.

LEAVING

EXT. NIGHT. THE STREETS OF TORONTO.

The Sarabande from Bach's *French Suite #1* is heard as we watch a black Lincoln Continental driving through a series of rainy, deserted streets late at night. It is the middle of a thunderstorm. We follow this car from the outside, looking in past the steady sweep of the wipers. We can only half make out the face of the driver through the wet windshield, over which the reflections of streetlamps, buildings and neon signs skitter nervously.

Glenn Gould is driving Long Fellow through deserted downtown Toronto. An erratic rhythm begins to emerge from this series of reflections. As the inside of the car is lit up, we briefly glimpse Gould's impassive face as he allows his car to be guided by the night.

EXT. NIGHT. DOWNTOWN.

Gould pulls the car into an alley and parks it haphazardly in front of a lone phone booth. The driver's side door is wide open and the dark, luxuriant music playing on the radio flows out to fill the barren urban landscape. A dark figure in a cloth raincoat is huddled over the phone, dialing. Glenn Gould is making a call.

> G.G.
> Hello Jessie, it's me. I was just out driving along and guess what came on the radio? Here ...

He holds the receiver outside of the booth so she can hear the music.

> G.G.
> Well? ... Yes, sure it's one of the French Suites, but which one? Here you go.

He holds out the receiver again.

The piece ends.

A BLACK SCREEN.

> RADIO ANNOUNCER
> [*voice*]
> And there you have it, Johann Sebastian Bach, the Sarabande from the *French Suite No. 1,* performed with the unmistakable genius of the young Glenn Gould. Tragically, Mr. Gould passed away this morning at the age of 50. He died in hospital in Toronto after suffering a stroke last week. Since that time, he'd been on a life-support system and never regained consciousness.

VOYAGER

STOCK FOOTAGE.

The Prelude in D Minor from Bach's *Nine Little Preludes* counterpoints NASA footage of a rocket lifting off. Viewed from above, in slow motion, the massive ship struggles free from the scaffolds and support lines that hold it to the earth.

ARIA
(Reprise)

EXT. DAY. A NORTHERN EXPANSE.

Once again we face the arctic desert. We hear the Prelude #1 from Bach's *Well-Tempered Clavier*—and someone reading.

Here it would seem that we are experiencing a memory. We see the exact sequence from the opening montage, but in reverse.

Glenn Gould passes by and then walks away from the camera. Further on, he turns to take a final look back at the world he is leaving. Implacably, he continues his journey until he has once again become a tiny, black dot at the centre of the frame.

G.G.

[*voice-over*]

In the fall of 1977, the U.S government sent two ships, Voyagers I and II, into space where they are eventually destinated to reach the edge of our galaxy. In the hope that someone, somewhere would intercept these craft, a variety of messages were placed on board that would be capable of communicating the existence of an intelligent creature living on a planet called Earth. Among these was included a short prelude by Johann Sebastian Bach, as performed by Glenn Gould. Voyagers I and II left our solar system respectively in 1987 and 1989.

CREDITS

A BLACK SCREEN.

As the credits slowly roll by, we hear Glenn Gould playing the Contrapuntus #9 from Bach's *The Art of the Fugue* on an organ.

Glenn Gould
Colm Feore

Director
François Girard

Producer
Niv Fichman

Screenplay
François Girard
Don McKellar

Director of Photography
Alain Dostie

Editor
Gaétan Huot

Line Producer
Amy Kaufman

1st Assistant Director
Jennifer Jonas

Casting
Deirdre Bowen

Cast
In order of appearance

Glenn Gould	Colm Feore
Gould's Father	Derek Keurvorst
Gould's Mother	Katya Ladan
Young Glenn age 3	Devon Anderson
Young Glenn age 8	Joshua Greenblatt
Young Glenn age 12	Sean Ryan
Chambermaid	Kate Hennig
Porter	Sean Doyle
Female Guide	Sharon Bernbaum
Concert Promoter	Don McKellar
Stagehand	David Hughes
C.B.S. Producer	Carlo D. Rota
C.B.S. Engineer	Peter Millard
C.B.S. Assistant Engineer	John Dolan
Waitress	Allegra Fulton
Trucker #1	Dick Callahan
Trucker #2	Guy Thauvette
Trucker #3	R.D. Reid
Trucker #4	Conrad Bergschneider
Music Critic	Gerry Quigley
Journalist	Gale Garnett
Writer	David Young
Photographer	James Kidnie
Girl	Maia Filar
Mother	Marina Anderson
Professor	Marie Josée Gauthier
Interpreter	Nick McKinney
Questioning Woman	Moynan King
VO Announcer	Knowlton Nash
Broker #1	Michael Kopsa

Broker #2	Len Doncheff
Phillip Brennan	Ian D. Clark
Desmond	David Clement
Waiter #1	Jimmy Loftus
Waiter #2	Frank Canino

Interviews

Bruno Monsaingeon	Sir Yehudi Menuhin
Margaret Pacsu	Jessie Greig

Interviews in Crossed Paths

Megan Smith	Walter Homburger
Ray Roberts	Bob Phillips
Jill R. Cobb	Bob Silverman
Elyse Mach	Mario Prizak
Valerie Verity	Vern Edquist

Opus #1 Performed by

Violin I	Bruno Monsaingeon
Violin II	Gilles Apap
Viola	Jean Marc Apap
Cello	Marc Coppey

Thirty-Two Short Films About Glenn Gould

Produced by
Rhombus Media Inc.

With the Participation of
Telefilm Canada
Ontario Film Development Corporation

In Association with
Canadian Broadcasting Corporation
Société Radio–Canada
NOS–Television
RTP–Portugal
OY Yleisradio AB (YLE)
The National Film Board of Canada
Glenn Gould Limited

Project Development	Jennifer Jonas
Research and Additional Writing	Nick McKinney
Research	Chantal Neveu
2nd Assistant Director	Leonard Farlinger
Production Co-ordinator	Karen Wookey
Script Supervisor	Leslie Druker
Design Consultant	Charles Dunlop
Associate Art Director	John Rubino
Set Decorator/Buyer	Alexa Anthony
Lead Set Dresser	Ian Nothnagel
Assistant Set Dressers	Doug McCullough
	Christopher Sharp
Property Master	Steve LeFave
Set Construction	Handmade Sets, Garfield
	Russell, John Moseley
Costume Designer	Linda Muir
Wardrobe Master	Derek Baskerville
Hairstylist	Marcelo Padovani
Make-up Artist	Kathryn Casault
Wigs	Gerald Altenburg
1st Assistant Cameraman	G. Chris Raucamp
Clapper/Loader	Dean Stinchcombe
Trainee	Jeremy Lyle
Stills Photography	Cylla von Tiedemann
Gaffer	David Owen
Best Boy Electric	Roscoe Kerr
Dailies	George Kerr
	Anthony Ramsey
Key Grip	Brian Potts
Best Boy Grip	Tom O'Riley
Dailies	Carl Savage
Location Sound	Stuart French
Boom Operator	Erika Schengili-Roberts
Location Manager	Alix Davis
Co-Unit Managers	John LaRose, Remo Girlato
Production Assistants	Stephen Butson, David
	Forsyth, J. Sam Straiton
Production Secretary	Naomi McCormack
Office Production Assistant	Sean Parker
Craft Services	Diana Seko

Catering	Blue Heron Catering, Om Taka Taka, One World Cuisine
Extras Casting	Scott Mansfield
Steadicam Operator	David Crone
Camera Car Operator	Canada Camera Car– Rick Leger
Vehicle Wrangler	Circle 'P' Ranch–Cactus Simser

2nd Unit – Montreal

Production Manager	Michel Siry
Assistant Camera	Paul Gravel
Location Sound	Daniel Masse
Production Assistant	Maurice Forget
Pixilation Camera	Sylvaine Dufaux
Assistant	Judith Gwendolyn Goulet

2nd Unit – Europe

Production Co-ordinator	Matthew Kitchen
Assistant Cameraman	Roger Hinrich
Location Sound	Gerard Dacquay

Post-Production

Post Production Co-ordination	Création Montage– Montreal
	Catherine Hunt–Toronto
Sound Editors	Jane Tattersall, John D. Smith
Assistant Sound Editor	Rich Harkness
Subtitles	Robert Gray
	Mary Ellen Davis
Re-Recording	Shelley Craig
Apprentice	Terry Mardini
Foley Artist	Andy Malcolm
Assistant	James A. Gore
Foley Recordist	Louis Hone
Video Transfers	Richard Lanoue
Timer	Gudrun Klawe
Negative Cutter	Claudine Blain, Diane Leroux
Titles	Louise Overy, Barry Wood
Photo Animation	Lynda Pelley, Pierre Landry

All piano music recordings by Glenn Gould
courtesy of Sony Classical GmbH

Aria
Aria from *The Goldberg Variations,* Johann Sebastian Bach
(recorded 1955).

Lake Simcoe
Overture from *Tristan and Isolde,* Richard Wagner. Performed by the
NBC Philharmonic Orchestra, conducted by Arturo Toscanini
(recorded 1952). Courtesy of BMG. Glenn Gould original
Chickering piano courtesy of CBC.

45 Seconds and a Chair
Two Part Invention #13 from *Two and Three Part Inventions,* Johann
Sebastian Bach. Based on an archival photograph by Don Hunstein.
Courtesy of Sony Classical GmbH.

Gould Meets Gould
Prelude from *English Suite #5,* Johann Sebastian Bach. Adapted from
an article in *High Fidelity,* February 1974. Used with the permission
of Hachette Magazines Inc. All rights reserved.

Hamburg
Allegro from *Sonata #13,* Ludwig van Beethoven.

Variation in C Minor
A variation from *32 Variations in C Minor,* Ludwig van Beethoven.
Optical printing by Luminefex.

Practice
Allegretto from *Sonata #17* (The Tempest), Ludwig van Beethoven.

L.A. Concert
Piano courtesy of Remenyi House of Music.

CD318
Prelude #2 from *The Well Tempered Clavier* (Volume 1), Johann
Sebastian Bach. Glenn Gould's piano courtesy of The National
Library of Canada. Piano played by Yuval Fichman.

Passion According to Gould
Gigue from *English Suite #2,* Johann Sebastian Bach. Authentic
Equipment courtesy of CBC Broadcast Museum, Coll Audio
Instruments Rental, Manta Sound.

Opus #1
Opus #1, Glenn Gould. Original Recording by Ed Visnovske, Sony
Classical Productions.

Crossed Paths
Adagio from *Sonata in B minor, Op.5,* Richard Strauss.

Truck Stop
Downtown, Tony Hatch. Performed by Petula Clark, Courtesy of
Welbec Music and Petula Clark, MCA Music Publishing. Trucks and
photos courtesy of Ross Mackie, Mackie Moving Systems.

The Idea of North
An excerpt from *The Idea of North,* Glenn Gould. Radio broadcast
aired December 28th, 1967. Courtesy of The Canadian Broadcasting
Corporation.

Solitude
Andantino from *Sonatina #2,* Jean Sibelius. Text from an interview
with Glenn Gould by Jonathan Cott, courtesy of Jonathan Cott.

Questions With No Answers
Prelude from *English Suite #2,* Johann Sebastian Bach.

A Letter
Variation #19 from *The Goldberg Variations,* Johann Sebastian Bach
(recorded 1955). Original letter courtesy of The National Library
of Canada.

Gould Meets McLaren
Fugue #14 from *The Well Tempered Clavier* (Volume 1), Johann
Sebastian Bach. An excerpt from *Spheres* by Norman McLaren and
René Jodoin, produced by The National Film Board
of Canada, 1969.

The Tip
Precipitato from *Sonata #7*, Sergei Prokofiev. Stock footage courtesy of The Canadian Broadcasting Corporation and The National Film Board of Canada.

Personal Ad
Désir from *Two Pieces Op. 57*, Alexander Scriabin.

Pills
Sehr lebhaft from *Sonata #3*, Paul Hindemith. Text taken from interviews conducted by Elyse Mach for *Great Pianists Speak for Themselves*. Courtesy of Dover Publications and Elyse Mach.

Diary of One Day
Gigue from *Suite for Piano Op.25*, Arnold Schoenberg. X-Ray equipment courtesy of Siemens Electric Ltd. X-Ray operation courtesy of Centre Hospitalier Universitaire de Sherbrooke. Irradiated people: Denis Bilodeau, Gilles Chouinard, Frank Desgagnés, Alain Dostie, François Girard, Jean-Pierre Girard, Jennifer Jonas, Pascale Landry, Michel Proulx, Jean-Louis Simard.

Motel Wawa
Ruhig bewegte Viertel from *Sonata #1*, Paul Hindemith. Text taken from interviews conducted by Elyse Mach for *Great Pianists Speak for Themselves*. Courtesy of Dover Publications and Elyse Mach.

Forty-Nine
Leicht Zart from *Six Little Pieces for Piano*, Arnold Schoenberg. Text adapted from 'Death in the Afternoon', by Glenn Gould, Week End Magazine, 1956.

Leaving
Sarabande from *French Suite #1*, Johann Sebastian Bach. Camera car provided by Canada Camera Car.

Voyager
Prelude in D Minor from *Nine Little Preludes*, Johann Sebastian Bach. Archival Footage of rocketry courtesy of Rudy Buttignol, Rudy Inc. NASA (National Aeronautics and Space Administration).

Aria
Prelude #1 from *The Well Tempered Clavier* (Volume 1), Johann
Sebastian Bach.

Credits
Contrapunctus #9 from *The Art of The Fugue,* Johann Sebastian Bach. Photo
of Glenn Gould by Don Hunstein, courtesy of Sony Classical GmbH.

The Producers gratefully acknowledge

Stéphane Blondin	Nicole Boutin
Barbara Brown	Jean Carpentier
Annie Cossette	Petula Clark
Atom Egoyan	Karen Franklin
Edgar Fruitier	Yolande Gervais
Herbert Gould	Jessie Greig
Ghislaine Guertin	Bruno Jobin
Professor Spiro Kizas	Tim Maloney

Sir Yehudi Menuhin

John Miller	Bruno Monsaingeon
Laurie Muretsky	Margaret Pacsu
Yves Pellerin	Michel Proulx
Stephen Posen	Ray Roberts
Jack Spears	Bob Trendholm
Lorne Tulk	Valerie Verity
Ed Visnovske	Garnet Willis
Stephen Willis	David Young

Casa Loma
CBC National News Library
Centre Hospitalier Universitaire de Sherbrooke
Frontier College, Toronto
The Glenn Gould Estate
Kodak, Canada
Massey Hall
Metropolitan Toronto Police
National Film Board of Canada
Staff of the National Library of Canada
Ontario Trucking Association
Panavision Montreal
Production Services

Riverdale Presbyterian Church
Royal Conservatory of Music
Senator Restaurant, Toronto
Siemens Electric Ltd.
Sommerville Leasing
Sony Classical Canada
The Toronto Symphony
University of Toronto
Vier Jahreszeiten Hotel, Hamburg
Jasper, Piaf, Sara and Tess

For Rhombus Media

Producers	Larry Weinstein
	Barbara Willis Sweete
Co-production Financing	Sheena Macdonald
Associate Producer	Daniel Iron
Office Co-ordinator	Brooke Weslak
Production Accountant	Linda Pope

For The National Film Board of Canada

Executive Producer	Dennis Murphy
Producer	Michael Allder
Technical Production Co-ordinator	Linda Payette
Business Manager	Ed Barreveld
Post Production Supervisor	Richard Michaud
Post Production Co-ordinator	Bryan Innes

International Distribution by
Sheena Macdonald, Rhombus International
Pierre Latour, Max Films International

A small picture of Glenn Gould scrolls centre frame, the only image of Gould in the film. It holds for a moment and fades.

Acknowledgements

The authors would like to thank Niv Fichman, friend and producer, Chantal
Neveu and Nick McKinney, tireless researchers, and Colm Feore, Alain Dostie,
Jennifer Jonas and Amy Kaufman, comrades in arms.

Thanks also to Stephen Posen, Ray Roberts and the Glenn Gould Foundation.

•

*Grateful acknowledgement is made to the following for permission to reprint
from previously published material:*
Elyse Mach. Excerpts from an interview with Glenn Gould from
Great Pianists Speak for Themselves, Dover Publications.
Reprinted by permission of Dover Publications, Inc.
Jonathan Cott. Excerpt from an interview with Glenn Gould, *Rolling Stone,*
Vol. 167. Reprinted by permission of the author.
Glenn Gould. Excerpt from 'Glenn Gould Interviews Glenn Gould
About Glenn Gould', *High Fidelity,* February 1974. Reprinted by
permission of Hachette Magazines Inc. All rights reserved.

•

The consent of the Glenn Gould Estate to the publication of
Thirty-Two Short Films About Glenn Gould is gratefully acknowledged.